Hugh Walker

Three Centuries of Scottish Literature

Vol. II

Hugh Walker

Three Centuries of Scottish Literature
Vol. II

ISBN/EAN: 9783337002411

Printed in Europe, USA, Canada, Australia, Japan

Cover: Foto ©Thomas Meinert / pixelio.de

More available books at **www.hansebooks.com**

THREE CENTURIES OF
SCOTTISH LITERATURE

BY

HUGH WALKER, M.A.

PROFESSOR OF ENGLISH IN ST. DAVID'S COLLEGE, LAMPETER

VOL. II

THE UNION TO SCOTT

Glasgow
JAMES MACLEHOSE AND SONS
PUBLISHERS TO THE UNIVERSITY
1893

CONTENTS OF VOLUME II.

.

THREE CENTURIES OF SCOTTISH LITERATURE.

CHAPTER VII.

RAMSAY TO FERGUSSON.

IN an earlier chapter reference has been made to the long and disastrous eclipse under which the native literature, and especially the poetry, of Scotland passed during the seventeenth century. The union of the Crown of Scotland with that of England would in any case have drawn talent from the smaller country; but if it had brought internal peace the loss would soon have been made good, and more than made good. But the Union did not bring peace. In the disturbed annals of Scotland there are periods of more violent commotion than the seventeenth century, but few if any more full of petty quarrels. Not only was the country shaken by the great civil struggle which convulsed England as well, but it was distracted also to a degree which England never experienced by religious differences. The mutual hatred of sects drained the strength of the nation; and on the whole it is little to be wondered at that there were only a few, like the Semples of Beltrees, who kept alive, in occasional compositions, the tradition of vernacular poetry.

As soon as the Revolution had effected a settlement, and the strong government of William, while justly establishing the Presbyterians as the exponents of the religion of the State, had prohibited the persecution of the now vanquished Episcopalians, literature and art began to revive. Some time had naturally to pass before the fruit of firm government and internal peace ripened ; and the literary revival is chronologically associated rather with the union of the Parliaments than with the Revolution. The removal of the seat of government to Westminster, if not a greater fact than the union of the Crowns, at any rate made a deeper and more permanent impression upon the literature of the smaller country. It was also different in its action. In the seventeenth century the leading poets, such as Sir William Alexander and Drummond of Hawthornden, Anglicised themselves as completely as they were able, and by doing so lost, to a large extent, their national audience. Vernacular literature seemed to be in danger of extinction. In the eighteenth century, on the contrary, an English and a Scottish school arose and flourished side by side. Further, the Scotchmen of the seventeenth century were almost wholly borrowers from the English ; they contributed no appreciable national element to the strong and healthy English literature of the reign of James I. Three generations later the case was very different. Not only the native school, but the Anglicised writers, taught at least as much as they learnt. They gave to a somewhat jaded literature a fresh impulse and a new vitality. In view of the condition of the literary society of Edinburgh in that age, this statement, as far as concerns the writers in English, may seem questionable. That society was organised in the closest imitation of that of London. Clubs sprang up where the wits assembled and sharpened their intellects one against another; periodicals were started to emulate *The Tatler* and *The Spectator*; and "correctness" was studied with as anxious care, though not with such conspicuous success, in the High Street and the Canongate as at Twickenham. And it is true that the minor writers of English are as little original as it is possible to conceive. With regard to the more considerable men, it will be the business of a separate chapter to justify the assertion that they taught as much as they learnt in England.

The first place in interest must however be given to the native school. It was original; for though Ramsay and his collaborateurs followed, they did not merely reproduce the old Scottish poetry, but adapted it to new circumstances and a new age. It was original so far, that the writers in it were among the earliest precursors of that revolution in poetic style which swept away the traditions of the "correct" poets, and established in their place the naturalism of Wordsworth. Many influences doubtless united to bring about that revolution; but the natural style was practised by Ramsay and his contemporaries, and after him by Fergusson, in Scotland, long before the principle of it was proclaimed in England. At the same time, the practice of these men was inconsistent. They apparently detected no incongruity between what they did in Scotch and what they did as imitators of Pope in English; probably they never brought the two styles of work together, tacitly assuming each to be proper in its own sphere.

The significance of Watson's *Choice Collection* has been already noted in connexion with the songs and ballads.

It gave a powerful stimulus to Scottish poetry in general, and especially to poetry in the vernacular; but, although part of the contents of the collection was new or recent, Watson brought to the front no hitherto unknown genius, no one who displayed a capacity for leadership, or who might have been expected to revive the poetic traditions of Dunbar and Douglas and Lindsay. William Hamilton of Gilbertfield was no more than respectable; yet he was the equal of any of the living writers whom Watson helped to bring forward. Five years passed between the beginning and the conclusion of Watson's undertaking— if that can be said to have a conclusion at all which ends with what was practically a promise, never fulfilled, of a new volume—and still no one had appeared of more than mediocre gifts. To the year after the appearance of Watson's third part, however, belong the earliest known verses of a man who, though not himself a great poet, did a great work for poetry. In 1712 the Easy Club was founded, and Allan Ramsay addressed it in a set of poor verses. He it was who was destined to breathe new life into Scottish vernacular poetry, and who in consequence holds a position inferior in historical interest only to that of Burns. He may be said, in fact, to have made Burns possible.

Allan Ramsay was born in the parish of Crawford-moor, a lonely district of Lanarkshire, in 1686. He was of good family, claiming kinship with the Ramsays of Dalhousie—

> " Dalhousie of an auld descent,
> My chief, my stoup, and ornament."

But the early death of his father and the remarriage of his mother left him to face the world poor and unassisted. In

1701 he was sent to Edinburgh as an apprentice to a wig-maker, whose trade he afterwards followed, until his literary tastes and connexions drew him into the more congenial one of bookselling. But, though Ramsay had genuine literary tastes, he was less a poet born than one made by circum-stances. He was social first, literary afterwards. The Easy Club, with its demand for occasional verses and its readiness to hear and applaud, gave him practice in composition and confidence in his own powers. Previous to his connexion with it Ramsay seems to have read little and written less. The club died in 1715; but, short as its life had been, his three years' attendance at its meetings had formed Ramsay's mind and determined his future life. He began to publish his verses as leaflets, which were sold in the streets of Edinburgh. It was as an editor, or more strictly as editor and author combined, that he made his first con-siderable venture. In 1716 appeared *Christ's Kirk on the Green*, in two cantos—the first a reprint of the old poem in the Bannatyne MS., the second an original addition. Soon afterwards a third canto, also by Ramsay, was added; and all three were published together in 1718. The success of this piece, which would have gratified many a man of older reputation, encouraged Ramsay to collect his own fugitive pieces into a volume, which came from the press of Ruddiman in 1721. The poet is said to have made 400 guineas by it, a large sum for those days. After an interval marked by some minor publications of original work, Ramsay appeared again as an editor. In 1724 he issued the first part of a most important collection of songs, *The Tea Table Miscellany*. Two other parts followed between that

date and 1727, and after a long interval a fourth was
added in 1740. The songs were a mixed collection,
vernacular and English, old and new. Some were by
Ramsay himself, some were the work of his literary
friends and correspondents; others were marked by him
as wholly old, or as old songs retouched. But the
object of *The Tea Table Miscellany* was to please
the public, not to instruct the inquirer into the history
of Scottish songs; and all who have ever handled it
with a historical object in view have had in consequence
to lament the vagueness and meagreness of the information supplied. Nothing is told but the bare fact that
a song is old, old with additions, or new—sometimes
not so much as that. In what way recovered, or how
old, or on what ground it was believed to be old, are
questions to which there is no answer in Ramsay. He
cannot however be blamed for not accomplishing what
he never attempted, or for being blind to that which
none of his contemporaries perceived. *The Tea Table
Miscellany*, faulty as it is from the point of view of
literary history, was and long remained without rival as a
collection of Scottish songs; and it has preserved much
that otherwise would probably have been lost. The
success of Ramsay too, encouraging others, like Oswald
and Thomson, to labour in the same field, led indirectly
to the recovery and preservation of other pieces.

In the same year in which the first part of *The Tea
Table Miscellany* appeared, Ramsay also published in two
small volumes a similar compilation, *The Evergreen*, which
he somewhat quaintly describes as "a collection of Scots
poems, wrote by the ingenious before 1600." The

materials for it were chiefly derived from the Bannatyne MS.; but they were treated uncritically and without that sense of responsibility and of obligation to accuracy with which the modern editor approaches such a task. Poems undoubtedly ancient are partly modernised, sometimes in a manner which proves that Ramsay did not understand the original; verses are here and there added by the editor's own hand; and the collection includes whole poems whose date is certainly long subsequent to 1600. Nevertheless, *The Evergreen* did its work for Ramsay's generation almost as well as a much more faithful reproduction of the old poems would have done. It furnished what men at that time really wished, and what it was important that they should have,—a knowledge of some of the hitherto unknown masterpieces of the great age of Scottish poetry. The editor's errors and sophistications were of little moment so long as the spirit of the poems he printed was not essentially changed; and the question whether his system of orthography had any authority outside himself was insignificant to men who had no inclination to investigate the history of the language. Ramsay himself had his taste trained, his knowledge widened, and his vocabulary enriched in the course of his labours as collector and editor; and this without opening to himself even the chance of falling into the errors of which his predecessors had been guilty. The best of those predecessors were in essence natural; but they had gathered to themselves a plentiful store of the affectations of a literary tradition. Their "aureate terms" were a snare exceedingly dangerous to the eighteenth century intellect and there can be little doubt that Ramsay would have gilded his own pages with them had he been able.   But the long break in the succession of poets saved him. Rhetoric is a growth.   No Euphues springs suddenly out of the void to talk his strange language to a wondering people; he must have forerunners.   But the rhetoric of Dunbar and Douglas had been in disuse for more than a century, and the sudden assumption of it by a living writer would not have pleased, but shocked.   Thus, while Ramsay in his English poems imitated as best he could the cultivated rhetoric of Pope, in those written in his native dialect he was forced to be plain and homely. And so, not through superior purity of taste, but by force of circumstances, Ramsay drew from the poetry of the sixteenth century all that was wholesome for his own age and rejected what would have been poisonous.

For some time Ramsay had been drifting in the direction of pastoral poetry.   There are to be found among his works a pastoral on the death of Addison, and another on the death of Prior, while one or two more were written to celebrate the marriage of distinguished persons.   These pieces are insignificant in themselves, and produced no such effect upon others as to give them importance by reflection.   But there were two, on subjects of his own imagining, which were much superior intrinsically and deeper in their influence.   These were *Patie and Roger*, published in 1721, and its sequel, *Jenny and Maggy*, which followed in 1723.   At the suggestion of friends they were worked up into *The Gentle Shepherd*, which is unquestionably the best of Ramsay's works, and unsurpassed in its own sphere in the English language.   It was published in 1725, became at once popular, and rapidly

passed through edition after edition. It was one of the
last of Ramsay's efforts in literature. In 1728 he published another volume of his poems, and in 1730 a collection of thirty *Fables*. Shortly afterwards he almost
entirely ceased to write. He was then the unchallenged
king of Scottish poets: he had become rich enough to
be independent of the profit derived from his books; and
he seems to have feared that perseverance might endanger
the fame he had already won. That he did not cease to
cherish his old interests is indicated by the fact that in
1736 he attempted to establish a theatre in Carrubber's
Close. But all that appertained to the stage still stank
in the nostrils of Scottish Presbyterianism; the theatre
was closed by order of the magistrates, and Ramsay sustained a heavy loss. His subsequent life was entirely
private. About 1755 he gave up business, and retired
to his house on Castle Hill. He died in 1758.

It remains to consider in more detail what manner of
poet this man was, who took up his craft, as it were, by
accident and dropped it at his pleasure. For any trace
of the inevitable in his verse the reader will look in
vain. The higher imagination was a gift denied to him;
yet with comparatively commonplace powers he exercised
an influence which many men far more richly endowed
have vainly striven to attain. It is to this, fully as much
as to the intrinsic worth of his verse, considerable as its
merit often is, that he owes his interest.

Of all Ramsay's works only one, *The Gentle Shepherd*,
covers more than a few pages. It is a pastoral, but a
pastoral with variations from the orthodox poetic type
which go far to explain the author's influence. No species

of poetry is more artificial than the pastoral. From the time of Theocritus it has been cast of set purpose in a conventional mould : the shepherds and their Arcadia are as far removed from this lower earth as the Utopia of the political dreamer. Many great poets in various tongues, and conspicuously Milton, had proved that this artificial form could be made the vehicle of profound and true poetry. But it was a dangerous style for a generation of poets already too conventional; and Pope and Philips show what it may become when the artificial framework is filled with artificial sentiment. Gay, who merely intended to produce a parody, did better than either of them; and Ramsay has more in common with him than with his more serious predecessors. The dramatic form of *The Gentle Shepherd* gives it freshness, and perhaps helps to keep the poet close to nature. He adopts, it is true, a number of conventionalities; the hero is a young laird brought up as a shepherd, the heroine a lady of high degree reared beside him as a shepherdess. But the spirit is unconventional. The scenery is a transcript from nature, the characters are genuine Scottish peasants, the actions part of the normal life of the people. The clothes-washing scene between Peggy and Jenny is as simple and true as that which Homer paints from a still more primitive society. In the conversation between Glaud and Symon, in the first scene of the second act, Ramsay enters into the details of the peasants' life with the confidence of one to whom it is familiar. The " peat ingle," the " divot seat," the ham " reesting in the nook," are things to be found nearer home than Arcadia. The harsher features of the shepherd's life are softened, as in a pastoral comedy they ought to be; yet they are not ignored. We hear of "blashy thows," and of the evils of storm and flood, but are not brought face to face with them. The atmosphere is one of humble plenty and content. The philosophy of the shepherd mind is expressed in the words of Patie :—

> " He that has just enough can soundly sleep;
> The o'ercome only fashes fowk to keep."

The style of *The Gentle Shepherd* is such as becomes the subject, simple and unambitious. It contains no lofty poetry, but a good deal of true humour and sympathetic delineation of character and life. The dialogue is sprinkled with songs, never of high merit, frequently of scarce moderate merit. Very often they simply weave into lyric measure the common sense of the conversation in which they are set; and therefore they are, as Ramsay's lyrics are apt to be, somewhat flat. But a defect of this kind is less serious there than it would have been in a work of a loftier strain. In *The Gentle Shepherd* Ramsay did not aim high, but he hit his mark. His comedy was at once recognised as genuine. It became a favourite with those whose life it portrays as well as with men of literary taste; and it takes rank amongst those works in which Scotland is rich beyond equal, works which not only treat of, but appeal to and are read by, the peasantry. It also gave a great impetus to the poetry of nature, was imitated by Ross in his *Helenore*, and exercised great influence over all writers in Scotch until Ramsay was superseded in popular favour by the higher genius of Burns.

The minor poems of Ramsay, though of only moderate

bulk, are most varied in kind. Humorous pieces, satires, elegiacs, fables and tales, songs in many keys, odes and addresses on anniversaries and ceremonial occasions, all find their place in his works. Their merit also runs through a considerable range. The worst of them are very poor ; the best are far from raising him to the rank of a great poet, but they give him a title to an honourable place among the minor bards. Ramsay is least happy when he is serious. Occasionally throughout his literary life, but most frequently in the earlier part of it, he wrote in English, and he seems to have felt it necessary to use that language in his serious compositions ; but he rarely handled it with success. His phraseology is full of Scotticisms, sometimes of the most ludicrously obvious description. His attempts at reproducing the verse of Pope in such pieces as *Tartana, On Content, Health*, etc., exhibit how deplorably a man of keen common sense and native shrewdness may fail in self-criticism. So too, Ramsay's serious elegies are hardly ever successful ; the only one indeed which can be called so is that on Newton, whose greatness Ramsay felt, and whom he mourns with dignity. He had not the neatness of phrase and grace of style necessary for a good elegy. It is only when he allows humour to season his English, and he rarely does so, that it is at all worthy of a place beside his Scotch. *The Morning Interview* is amusing and clever, though it can ill stand comparison with *The Rape of the Lock*, of which it is an imitation.

The use of Scotch in Ramsay's serious poems is exceptional ; but in one conspicuous instance, *The Vision*, he does resort to it in a sober and even elevated frame of mind. It was one of those published in *The Evergreen* as of ancient composition; but it has been proved beyond reasonable doubt that the verses are Ramsay's. In the poet's own day, as one of his biographers suggests, it would have been injudicious, and perhaps dangerous, to own the Jacobitical sentiments, which under a thin veil he there allows to appear. *The Vision* is a more ambitious effort than almost any other which Ramsay ever made. Its ostensible subject is the national struggle for independence against Edward I. The Scotch version which Ramsay gives does not profess to be so old as that. According to a note attached to it in *The Evergreen*, it was first written in Latin in 1300, and translated in 1524; but the language is certainly not the language of the first half of the 16th century, though the desire to imitate it gives the piece an air of antiquity. The poet pictures himself wandering about musing on the misfortunes of his country, when a sudden May storm drives him to seek shelter under a caverned rock. There he falls asleep, and in vision sees the warden of the nation, who holds converse with him, denouncing the treachery of the peers which has brought Scotland to her state of thraldom, and prophesying the brighter future which is to dawn with Bruce. In this loftier strain Ramsay is successful to a degree that could scarcely have been expected. *The Vision* manifests power of imagination, force of language, and nobility of sentiment. But it exhibits also characteristic defects. The versification is extremely uneven, perhaps in mistaken imitation of the older style; and the stanzas on the carousals of the gods present a picture odiously vulgar, and altogether out of place. The following vigorous description of the storm is a specimen

of the better qualities of the poem, not without some
trace of its faults :—

> " The air grew ruch with bousteous thuds ;
>   Bauld Boreas branglit outthrow the cluds,
>   Maist lyke a drunken wicht ;
>   The thunder crakt, and flauchts did rift,
>   Frae the blak vissart of the lift ;
>   The forest shuke with fricht ;
>   Nae birds abune thair wing extenn,
>   They ducht not byde the blast ;
>   Ilk beast bedeen bang'd to their den,
>   Until the storm was past :
>   Ilk creature, in nature,
>   That had a spunk of sense,
>   In neid then, with speid then,
>   Methocht, cry'd in defence."

The following stanza pictures the warden of Scotland :—

> " Grit darring dartit frae his ee,
>   A braid-sword shogled at his thie,
>   On his left arm a targe ;
>   A shynand speir fill'd his richt hand,
>   Of stalwart mak in bane and brawnd,
>   Of just proportions, large ;
>   A various rainbow-colourt plaid
>   Owre his left spaul he threw :
>   Doun his braid back, from his quhyt heid,
>   The silver wymplers grew.
>   Amaisit, I gaisit,
>   To se, led at command,
>   A stampant, and rampant,
>   Ferss lyon in his hand."

It will be not unprofitable to compare with this the well-
known verses in which Burns in his *Vision* depicts the
greatness of his country, especially as the more recent
poet had his predecessor in his mind.   The comparison
shows how high the work of a truly great poet towers

above even the happier efforts of inferior powers. Burns effects his purpose less directly than Ramsay in the description of Coila's plaid :—

> " Here, rivers in the sea were lost ;
> There, mountains to the skies were tost ;
> Here, tumbling billows mark'd the coast
>   With surging foam ;
> There, distant shone Art's lofty boast,
>   The lordly dome.

> " Here, Doon pour'd down his far-fetched floods ;
> There, well-fed Irwine stately thuds ;
> Auld hermit Ayr staw thro' his woods,
>   On to the shore,
> And many a lesser torrent scuds,
>   With seeming roar.

> " By stately tow'r or palace fair,
> Or ruins pendent in the air,
> Bold stems of heroes, here and there,
>   I could discern ;
> Some seem'd to muse, some seem'd to dare,
>   With feature stern."

The buffoonery, which is the darkest blot on Ramsay's *Vision*, betrays a want of taste which always clung to him, and which of itself was enough to put success in the higher walks of poetry beyond his reach. *Lochaber No More*, the loftiest of his lyrics, is likewise marred by a deformity which may be of kindred origin. Everyone who is familiar with the song must be sensible of the ludicrous effect of the lines in which the hero excuses his tears :—

> " These tears that I shed they are a' for my dear,
> And no for the danger attending on wear."

Professor Minto charitably supposes that they must have been dictated by "the humorous imp that was Ramsay's true familiar." But whether intentional or unconscious, the incongruity, degrading a song otherwise fine though not otherwise faultless, is equally inexcusable.

But as Ramsay was little fitted to excel in serious composition, so his literary creed subjected him to no temptation to strive after the unattainable. He was fired by no grand conception of the dignity of his office, and as a caterer to the popular amusement was ready to acquiesce in the popular judgment:—

> " If happily you gain them to your side,
>   Then bauldly mount your Pegasus and ride :
>   Value yourself what only they desire ;
>   What does not take, commit it to the fire."

Acting upon this creed, Ramsay found that he could please best by giving way to his own natural disposition. As to what that disposition was he leaves the reader in no doubt ; for his simple, easy confidences are among the charms of his verse. He is " mair to mirth than grief inclined." He hates drunkenness and gluttony, but is " nae fae to wine and mutton." His very physical appearance is recorded as faithfully as his predilections :—

> " Imprimis, then, for tallness, I
>   Am five foot and four inches high ;
>   A black-a-vic'd, snod, dapper fallow,
>   Nor lean nor overlaid with tallow."

His social philosophy is accurately described in lines which, though not really Ramsay's, are usually printed among his works. They are to be found in *Pills to Purge Melancholy ;* but as they are valuable to illustrate Ramsay, and as moreover he has some claim upon them through changing, expanding, and improving the original, they may be quoted :—

> " See that shining glass of claret,
>   How invitingly it looks !
> Take it aff, and let's have mair o't,
>   Pox on fighting, trade, and books.
> Let's have pleasure while we're able,
>   Bring us in the meikle bowl,
> Place 't on the middle of the table,
>   And let wind and weather growl.

> " Call the drawer, let him fill it
>   Fou as ever it can hold ;
> O tak tent ye dinna spill it,
>   'Tis mair precious far than gold.
> By you've drunk a dozen bumpers,
>   Bacchus will begin to prove,
> Spite of Venus and her mumpers,
>   Drinking better is than love."

Such was Ramsay in real life—a kindly, easy-going, but at the same time acute and sensible man of clubs and convivial gatherings. All his best work in the minor poems was such as a man of this description could do. Add sympathy, and *The Gentle Shepherd* also is explained. He scourged the vices of his own time and his own country, sometimes with a coarseness which bars quotation, but generally with energy and effect. He held and commonly acted upon the sensible theory that satire ought to forbear that which is quite contemptible—" 'Tis fools in something wise that satire claim "; and the objects of his satire are either the errors of a class or of the nation, or of individuals as

representative of classes.   From spite and malevolence
Ramsay is free.

It is however where the satire is strongly spiced with
humour or in pieces purely humorous that Ramsay is
at his best.   The elegy on *John Cowper*, the Kirk-
treasurer's man, is just such a subject as suits him.
The Kirk-treasurer's man played the part of police in
the enforcement of that extraordinary ecclesiastical discipline which, from its institution till the change of
manners first modified and afterwards abolished it, had
to be reckoned with by evil-doers.   They found it a
most disagreeable reality; but at all times it was a reality
which lent itself easily to jest and ridicule; and perhaps
there were balm to the smart in turning the laugh against
the executioner.   If Ramsay had no personal quarrel with
Kirk Sessions, as Burns had in after times, he was the mouth-
piece of many a one who had.   The elegies on *Maggie
Johnstoun* and *Lucky Wood* are pitched to a similar key.
They are full of references to convivial customs which bring
clearly before the mind the image of a society in which
drunkenness was respectable in all and normal in many.
The game of hy-jinks, which regulated a man's drinking
by the throw of the dice, and the club of "facers," who
pledged themselves to throw in their own faces all they
left in the glass, could only have thriven in such a
society.   The cantos in which Ramsay continued *Christ's
Kirk on the Green* gave him the opportunity of dis-
playing the same merits on a wider field.   The old
poet having depicted a rustic fight, Ramsay carries a
like spirit into rustic revelry and mirth; and it is no
mean praise to say that the continuation is not un-

worthy of the original. For broad riotous fun it has rarely been surpassed. But Ramsay's work is coarser than the old poem, and there is evident in it an element of vulgarity not to be found in the model, though the latter deals with the same class of people and handles them as fearlessly and apparently with as full knowledge. *The Monk and the Miller's Wife* would claim notice in this context; but, as it is simply the old tale of the *Freiris of Berwick* modernised, its high merits should be ascribed, not to Ramsay, but to the author of that tale.

In the songs there may be seen once and again evidences of similar powers under similar limitations. Though in his influence upon Scottish song Ramsay is second only to Burns, he owes this influence to circumstances more than to the quality of his verse. Many have written better than he. The man who cannot compose twenty lines of heroic sentiment without ruining them, whether of purpose or unwittingly, with mean images or vulgar description, can never be a great lyrist; for however admirable a humorous lyric may be, it remains true that "our sweetest songs are those that tell of saddest thought." Occasionally Ramsay does well; but not once is he able to tune his heart to the noblest and clearest notes of passion. *An thou wert my ain thing* is a favourable specimen; but it is clear that the author never lost himself in his subject. *The Young Laird and Edinburgh Katy* is excellent. It breathes a strong sense of the beauties of nature :—

> "O Katy ! wiltu gang wi' me,
>   And leave the dinsome town a while?

> The blossom's sprouting frae the tree,
>   And a' the simmer's gaun to smile ;
> The mavis, nightingale, and lark,
>   The bleating lambs and whistling hynd,
> In ilka dale, green, shaw, and park,
>   Will nourish health, and glad ye'r mind.

> " There's up into a pleasant glen,
>   A wee piece frae my father's tower,
> A canny, saft, and flow'ry den,
>   Which circling birks has form'd a bower :
> Whene'er the sun grows high and warm,
>   We'll to the cawler shade remove ;
> There will I lock thee in mine arm,
>   And love and kiss, and kiss and love."

Even this beautiful song however is spoilt by a hatefully affective phrase, "the clear goodman of day."

Ramsay's mind is better illustrated in *Bessy Bell and Mary Gray* than in the foregoing lines. The manner in which he has treated their story is most instructive. The old ballad was tragic ; Ramsay turns it into comedy—comedy which is both clever and amusing, but not poetical. The idea of a lover at a loss to determine between two equally attractive beauties may be expressed at least as well in prose as in verse, and was expressed many centuries ago, in generalised shape, in fable. It is a favourite with Ramsay. He repeats it, and manages it with equal success, in *Genty Tibby and Sonsy Nelly.* But perhaps the best of his lighter songs is one in praise of drinking, *Up in the Air* :—

> " Now the sun's gane out o' sight,
>   Beet the ingle, and snuff the light ;
> In glens the fairies skip and dance,
>   And witches wallop o'er to France ;

Up in the air
On my bonny grey mare,
And I see her yet, and I see her yet,
Up in the air
On my bonny grey mare,
And I see her yet, and I see her yet.

" The wind's drifting hail and snaw
O'er frozen bogs like a footba';
Nae starns keek thro' the azure slit,
'Tis cauld and mirk as ony pit:
The man i' the moon
Is carousing aboon,
D'ye see, d'ye see, d'ye see him yet?
The man i' the moon, etc.

" Take your glass to clear your een,
'Tis the elixir heals the spleen,
Baith wit and mirth it will inspire,
And gently puff the lover's fire,
Up in the air,
It drives away care,
Hae wi' ye, hae wi' ye, and hae wi' ye, lads, yet.
Up in the air, etc.

" Steek the doors, keep out the frost,
Come, Willy, gie's about ye'r toast ;
Tilt it, lads, and lilt it out,
And let's hae a blythsome bowt ;
Up wi't there, there,
Dinna cheat, but drink fair ;
Huzza, huzza, and huzza ! lads, yet.
Up wi't there, etc."

Ramsay is master of another note which is perhaps his
best. When his rollicking conviviality is tempered by a
spirit of seriousness betraying the shrewd man of the
world and the successful man of business, he develops an
Epicurean philosophy not unlike that of Horace. A
sound instinct sent him to Horace as his exemplar. He

himself was not artist enough to blend grave and gay harmoniously together, and to cause deep conviction and the practical wisdom resulting from ripe experience to manifest themselves 'beneath the guise of careless gaiety; but he found in the Roman poet the guidance which he needed, and he used him with remarkable skill, keeping him, as he has himself explained, or dropping him as he pleased.   His best performance in this mood is an ode in which he paraphrases and expands Horace, Od. I. 9; and it is in this and a few similar pieces that the real Ramsay stands revealed :—

> " Look up to Pentland's towering tap,
>   Buried beneath great wreaths of snaw,
>   O'er ilka cleugh, ilk scar, and slap,
>   As high as ony Roman wa'.
>
> " Driving their baws frae whins to tee,
>   There's no nae gowfer to be seen,
>   Nor dousser fowk wysing a-jee,
>   The byast bouls on Tamson's green.
>
> " Then fling on coals, and ripe the ribs,
>   And beik the house baith but and ben,
>   That mutchkin stoup it hads but dribs,
>   Then let's get in the tappit hen.
>
> " Good claret best keeps out the cauld,
>   And drives away the winter soon;
>   It makes a man baith gash and bauld,
>   And heaves his saul beyond the moon.
>
> " Leave to the gods your ilka care,
>   If that they think us worth their while,
>   They can a' rowth of blessings spare,
>   Which will our fasheous fears beguile.
>
> " For what they hae a mind to do,
>   That will they do, should we gang wud;

If they command the storms to blaw,
    Then upo' sight the hailstanes thud.

" But soon as e'er they cry, 'Be quiet,'
    The blatt'ring winds dare nae mair move,
But cour into their caves and wait
    The high command of supreme Jove.

" Let neist day come as it thinks fit,
    The present minute's only ours ;
On pleasure let 's employ our wit,
    And laugh at Fortune's feckless powers.

" Be sure ye dinna quat the grip
    Of ilka joy when ye are young,
Before auld age your vitals nip,
    And lay ye twafald o'er a rung.

" Sweet youth 's a blyth and heartsome time ;
    Then, lads and lasses, while it 's May,
Gae pou the gowan in its prime,
    Before it wither and decay.

" Watch the saft minutes o' delyte
    When Jenny speaks beneath her breath,
And kisses, laying a' the wyte
    On you, if she kep ony skaith.

" 'Haith, ye're ill-bred '; she'll smiling say,
    ' Ye'll worry me, you greedy rook.'
Syne frae your arms she'll rin away,
    And hide hersell in some dark nook.

" Her laugh will lead you to the place
    Where lies the happiness you want,
And plainly tells you to your face,
    Nineteen nay says are half a grant.

" Now to her heaving bosom cling,
    And sweetly toolie for a kiss,
Frae her fair finger whop a ring,
    As taiken of a future bliss.

" These benisons, I'm very sure,
    Are of the gods' indulgent grant,
Then, surly carles, whisht, forbear
    To plague us with your whining cant."

Such was the man who holds the position of leader in the Scottish poetical revival of the eighteenth century. He had predecessors, indeed he was so little of an original genius that he would probably never have written had there not been a popular demand for the kind of verse he supplied. The language of political economy is well applied to it, for there never was a clearer case in literature of the operation of economic laws. But except Ramsay, there was no one who displayed any sustained capacity to furnish what was wanted. There were numbers who could write an occasional piece tolerably well, but few who could be trusted to succeed in numerous efforts. Among the living contributors to Watson's *Choice Collection* there was none of higher merit than William Hamilton of Gilbertfield, who simply did what numbers have done since and are doing now unnoticed—he wrote two or three fugitive pieces, vigorously expressed and enlivened by a certain gift of humour, genuine but not very deep.

The facts of Hamilton's life are, as is the case with so many Scottish poets, but obscurely known. He died in 1751 at a great age, but the exact date of his birth has not been discovered. He had been a soldier, but abandoned his profession while still young, and subsequently lived the leisurely life of a country gentleman, amusing himself from time to time by writing verses. Commonplace as he is, in the "dearth of fame" Hamilton deserves to be commemorated. He cannot be called Ramsay's disciple, inasmuch as he had written his best verses before the other had done more than dream of a literary career, if his practical mind ever indulged in dreams on the subject. Nevertheless, he owes to the younger poet the greater part of such reputation as he possesses, both because it was the reflection of Ramsay's fame which gave significance to the contemporary contributions to Watson, and more directly because Hamilton and Ramsay entered into a poetical correspondence through which the verses of the former, which are printed along with Ramsay's works, have become known to a wider audience than he ever addressed on his own account. The correspondence is further noteworthy because it became a model for the familiar epistles of Burns. It has been affirmed that Hamilton's share in it is at least equal in quality to Ramsay's, a compliment which, as the contributions of the more famous poet are very ordinary, is not in itself extravagant, but which nevertheless goes beyond the truth. Hamilton's epistles are even less than fair specimens of a style of poetry which never, except in the hands of Burns, rises much above the commonplace. In the same measure, and in a similar tone of familiar, humorous, vernacular verse, was written Hamilton's best piece, *The Last Dying Words of Bonny Heck*, the lament of a famous greyhound, which was printed in the *Choice Collection*. It has considerable force and is not without humour; but the degree of attention it attracted is only explicable by reference to the scarcity of genuine native poetry at the time of its appearance. Ramsay affected to class it with *The Piper of*

Kilbarchan, "standart Habby," as the model on which he based his own attempts in that measure; but there is a power and freedom in the older piece which Hamilton could never approach. It would have been well had Hamilton confined himself to original efforts, which were generally meritorious and at worst harmless. Unfortunately, three years after his correspondence with Ramsay (which occurred in 1719), he appeared in a new character, as the editor of an ill-executed and discreditable modernised version of Blind Harry's *Wallace*. The popularity which this version attained was due, not to its merits, but to the irresistible attractions of the subject for the Scottish peasantry.

Another Hamilton, William Hamilton of Bangour—sometimes confounded with Hamilton of Gilbertfield, to whom he was junior by a whole generation—rose into prominence soon after this, and must be noticed in his place; but although he has been ranked [1] as a scholar of Ramsay, his true affinities are with the English school. In fact, Ramsay had no immediate followers of note. There were many who were ready to contribute an occasional song to *The Tea Table Miscellany*, men of talent with literary proclivities but with no purpose of devoting themselves to literature, and with too much ambition to confine themselves, had they done so, to the scanty audience supplied by Scotland itself. The clubs, which formed one of the most remarkable features of the age, were inimical in spirit to the vernacular. Ready though they were to welcome and applaud the occasional verses of Ramsay, they were too directly imitations of the

[1] By Mr. Gosse, *Eighteenth Century Literature*, p. 338.

literary societies of the English capital to escape being
Anglicised. Their members therefore neither wrote much
in Scotch nor were careful to claim property in what they
did write. Their identity is generally but half revealed
through initials; and though in most cases the disguise
may be penetrated, the quantity of matter associated with
any single name is so small that it becomes necessary to
treat their work *en bloc.* Further, it must be remembered
that, large as is the collection called by Ramsay
The Tea Table Miscellany, it is "a collection of choice
songs Scots and English"; and the word "English" here
must be understood in a double sense. The element
which is English in origin as well as in language is
much more considerable than is generally supposed; its
extent can only be realised after a careful examination
of the contents by one tolerably familiar with both
English and Scotch lyric poetry, not of that age only,
but for a generation or two previous. Again, many of
those songs which are the genuine work of Scottish
authors, many even of those which are also set to native
airs, are influenced by English models. Damon, Strephon,
Celia, Phillis, and Chloe are no maids and swains of
Scottish growth; nor did those who sang of them north
of the Tweed follow native example. Even when the
theme and all its associations are distinctively Scotch, it
is comparatively rare among the new songs in that collection to find the vernacular employed by anyone except
Ramsay himself. In *The Bush aboon Traquair*, in his
much over-praised *Tweedside*, in *Allan Water*, in the *Rose
in Yarrow*, and even in *Down the Burn, Davie*, Robert
Crawford, one of the most trusty of Ramsay's associates,

employs language which is either pure English or has only the least tincture of Scotch.

And where Ramsay's immediate following in lyric verse was slight, in efforts more sustained it was scarcely to be expected that he would find a following at all. The composition in Scotch of a long piece like *The Gentle Shepherd* was an innovation so bold that Ramsay would probably not have risked it had the plan occurred to him all at once. It grew, as has been seen, under his hand; and it was less venturesome to fashion the whole out of previously existent fragments than to create a new work on such a scale. No less than forty-three years passed before *The Gentle Shepherd* was followed by another poem equally ambitious in the same language. That poem is *Helenore, or The Fortunate Shepherdess*, published at Aberdeen in 1768, but written, as the advertisement to the first edition[1] states, many years before. The author was Alexander Ross, a schoolmaster, who was born in 1699 at Kincardine-O'Neil in Aberdeen-shire, and received his university education at Marischal College. After taking his degree in 1718 he acted for a time as a private tutor, and afterwards taught successively in the parish schools of Aboyne and Laurence-kirk. In 1732 he was appointed schoolmaster of Lochlee in Forfarshire, a place so lonely that only the children of some five or six families attended his school. This humble preferment was the last he received. At Lochlee he lived and died, and there on the scanty income of his office he reared a numerous family. Doubtless the profound quiet and abundant leisure of his life fostered the

[1] Quoted by Longmuir, *Life of Ross*, p. 49.

literary tendencies of Ross. He wrote apparently more for his own amusement than with any definite purpose of publishing. His verses circulated in MS.; he acquired a local reputation as a poet; and it was after that reputation had been long and firmly established that he determined to try how the world would receive him. Accordingly he visited Aberdeen in 1766 with the MS. of *The Fortunate Shepherdess* in his pocket. There he saw Beattie, who, although he had not yet risen to the height of his repu-tation, was already known as a poet, and was one of the most influential of the members of the remarkable literary coterie which then adorned the northern University. Beattie, attracted to Ross by the memory of an old friendship between his father and the poet, helped the aspirant for poetic fame over the difficulties of publi-cation. Nor did his kindness stop there. He gave the book generous praise, and even addressed to the author, through the pages of *The Aberdeen Journal*, a poetical epistle in Scotch, his only composition in dialect. Thus befriended, Ross's poem speedily attained that popularity which it certainly merited, but which might otherwise have been more slow to come, and a measure of financial success, modest enough (the profits amounted to about £20), but more than sufficient to satisfy the author. The rustic poet found himself, in a more limited way, and for a time, patronised by the great as Burns was afterwards; but he speedily subsided again into the old quiet life of Lochlee, and notwithstanding the encouragement given by the reception of his pastoral, the bulk of his writings remained, and still remain, in MS. He died at Lochlee in 1784.

Helenore is a pastoral narrative poem of over 4000

lines. The poet begins with an invocation to his muse, Scota, whom Burns in a letter declares to be the original from which he took his Coila. Scota however has none of the imaginative attributes of Coila. She listens to her poet, promises him a modest share of inspiration, but at the same time warns him that her "ain bairn," Ramsay, to whom Ross had referred as his model, is raised high above aught that he may aspire to reach. The poem, over the creation of which the muse is called upon to preside, is a singular mixture of true naturalness and simplicity with a superficial show of artificiality. Its principal incidents, though they are and long have been so impossible as to suggest a remote antiquity, were familiar enough to the minds of all the poet's contemporaries; and, though apparently then unknown in his immediate neighbourhood, they were within the experience of some of his countrymen. The shepherds, the manner of their existence, and the scenes amidst which they live, are all real. In these points and in all essentials Ross is as faithful to nature as Ramsay. But his system of names is as incongruous as any that a perverted taste ever devised. Chloe and her sisterhood are objectionable even in a song; but in a long work dealing with the lives and actions of northern rustics, names like Helenore, Rosalind, and Olimund are insufferable. The familiar abbreviations, Nory, Lindy, and Mundy, though they doubtless indicate a lurking sense of incongruity in the mind of Ross, do not mend matters. In this ridiculous piece of affectation we have probably a mark of the pedagogue's taste, and a relic of his unwillingness to sink the scholar in the popular poet.

But notwithstanding superficial absurdities and faults of a deeper if less obtrusive description, *Helenore* is a poem of very considerable merit. The scene is laid on the border between Lowland civilisation and what was still Highland savagery : on just that meeting ground of two races and of two types of scenery whose wealth of picturesque situation Scott perceived so clearly and utilised in *The Lady of the Lake* and in *Waverley*. Ross's choice however was not determined by the considerations which moved Scott, nor was he to any considerable extent alive to his opportunities. It is true that the contrasts of scenery are not unskilfully managed ; the wild loneliness of the mountain whose sounds are the cries of the earnbleater and the muirfowl, and whose sights are a succession of "dens and burns and braes and langsome moors," in opposition to the gentle streams, the bleating flocks, and the wooded slopes of the richer lowland. In every reference to scenery Ross is true, because he copies nature ; but it is only the cultivated country, Flaviana, that he depicts with affection :—

> " The water feckly on a level sled,
>   Wi' little dinn, but couthy what it made,
>   On ilka side the trees grew thick and strang,
>   And wi' the birds they a' were in a sang :
>   On ev'ry side, a full bow-shot and mair,
>   The green was even, gowany, and fair ;
>   With easy sklent, on ev'ry hand the braes,
>   To right well up, wi' scatter'd busses raise :
>   Wi' goats and sheep aboon, and ky below,
>   The bonny braes a' in a swarm did go."

The wilder Highland scenery is as a dark background to this picture. It is not dwelt upon with affection or with that stirring of the spirit which indicates that the sense of sublimity is awakened, but is accepted as a disagreeable fact.

The same is true with regard to the characters. The Sevitians play a conspicuous part in the story; for it is by their irruption into the peaceful glen that the fortunes of hero and heroine are changed. Rosalind (the name is masculine in Ross) and Helenore are shepherd and shepherdess living in Flaviana and moving towards the orthodox destiny, when an inroad of Kettrin occurs, in resisting which Rosalind is taken, while Helenore is lost in seeking to discover him. The issue is most unpoetical. Ross is tempted by the glitter of squiredom to make the severance of the pair permanent. Helenore in her wanderings meets a gentleman who falls in love with her; and, to remove every objection, it is discovered that she is related to him. Rosalind on his part buys his freedom by promising marriage to a damsel of the Sevitians named Bydby, and is afterwards forced most unwillingly to keep his word. Bydby is the only Sevitian who is individually depicted; and even in her case there is no attempt to mark her by the characteristics of her race. Her countrymen are, like their mountains, only a background to the shepherd population among whom Ross lived.

The meanness which is visible in the *dénouement* of the story is indicative of the limitation of Ross's poetical faculty. There is little in him of "the consecration and the poet's dream." His is a matter-of-fact mind: he tells the reader plainly of the nausea which afflicts both his principal female characters from eating berries in their wanderings among the hills. But this, which is his weakness, is at the same time his strength. He is always true. Even in his unfortunate conclusion he is only depicting, perhaps a little too faithfully, the ambitions of the class from which his characters are drawn—ambitions which after all do not differ in kind from those cherished in higher ranks of life. It has even been suggested that the story of *Helenore* was probably based on fact, and that the infidelity may not have been of Ross's invention.[1] At any rate, if he is destitute of some of the virtues which are always expected and generally found in pastoral poetry, he possesses others which are extremely rare. His narrative is vigorous, the interest well sustained, and the characters of the shepherd people not ill-drawn. In these respects Ross followed, and followed well, his master Ramsay. He added however little to what Ramsay had done. His powers were in the main similar, and they were less considerable.

Helenore is by no means the only work of Ross; the mass of his unpublished writings much exceeds that of the portion which has seen the light. So far as can be judged from the account given by Longmuir of the inedited works, they are not of a character greatly to increase his reputation. *The Fortunate Shepherd, or the Orphan* was clearly prompted by the success of *Helenore*. A translation in prose of Buchanan's *De Jure* and another in verse of Ramsay's *Poemata Sacra* exhibit Ross's scholarly interests, and probably indicate the direction in which his ambition set. An attempt to throw the book of Job into English verse casts suspicion on his judgment as well

[1] Longmuir, p. 117.

as his modesty; and the singular production entitled
A Dream, in imitation of the Cherry and the Slae, betrays
the limitation of his skill in versification.   The compli-
cated measure of the old poem overstrains the powers of
Ross; and Montgomery, whom he sees in his dream,
graciously permits him to change it.   Besides all these,
Ross was the author of a small but excellent collection
of songs which display him in a new and unexpected
light.   *The Rock and the wee pickle Tow, To the begging
we will go*, and *Woo'd an' Married an' a'*, are probably
the best things he ever wrote.   They have more *verve*
than *Helenore*, and they are rich in a humour not to
be found in it.   Ross seems to be inspired by the
genuine spirit of the old Scottish songs, his imagination
brightens, his vocabulary grows richer, and the verses
he writes in this spirit are among the best prior to
Burns.

As Ross was the first true successor of Ramsay in the
sphere of the pastoral, so was Robert Fergusson the first
real inheritor of the humorous and satiric power of his
epistles, mock elegies, and tales.   Fergusson's name is of
interest because of a story only less pathetic than that
of Chatterton, and also because he was in a special sense
the precursor and early model of Burns.   Fergusson was
the son of an Edinburgh clerk, and was born in that
city in 1750.   Though his father was very poor, his total
income amounting for a long time to only about £25 a
year, he contrived to give his son a good education.
After four years at the Edinburgh High School the boy
secured a Fergusson bursary, under the terms of which
he had to remove to the Grammar School of Dundee.

Thence he passed, as required by the bequest under which he was being educated, to St. Andrews University, where he matriculated in February, 1765. He won there the friendship of Wilkie of *The Epigoniad*, and on the whole seems to have borne a fair reputation, notwithstanding the fact that in March, 1768, he was "extruded" for complicity in some boyish breach of discipline. As he was readmitted four days later, his offence cannot have been considered very serious. At the end of the session in which this occurred, Fergusson left the University and returned to Edinburgh to live with his mother, by this time a widow. Pressed by poverty, but without any personal regrets, he abandoned the purpose of studying for the Church, and in 1769, as the readiest way of earning a living, became a clerk in the office of Charles Abercromby, Commissary-Clerk. The ceaseless drudgery of transcription, for that was the nature of his work, was very little to his taste; and it was but natural that he should look beyond the walls of his employer's office for mental and physical recreation. He had been from an early date a scribbler of verse. There is still to be found among his works an *Elegy on the Death of Mr. David Gregory*, written, it may be presumed, when the event, which occurred in April, 1765, was recent. But his poetic vein was little worked before the year 1771, when he began to contribute to Ruddiman's *Weekly Magazine, or Edinburgh Amusement*. At first there seems to have been a danger that he would become merely the commonplace writer of commonplace stanzas in imitation of the English poets; but though too much of his energy was thus squandered, some part of it was fortunately reserved for those poems in Scotch through which alone his name is memorable.

His poetical contributions to the *Magazine* speedily won for Fergusson a reputation in Edinburgh literary society; and in October, 1772, following the almost universal drift of the times, he became a member of an association known as the Cape Club. He was not able to resist the temptations to excess which society in those days presented; but if ever excess was pardonable, Fergusson's may be forgiven: "Anything," he exclaimed, "to forget my poor mother and these aching fingers." His literary efforts did something to better his circumstances. He was paid for his contributions to Ruddiman's paper; and when they had grown sufficiently numerous he reissued them, in 1773, as a separate volume. By this venture he is said to have cleared over £50, a very considerable sum for him. An analysis of the contents of the volume is interesting. It contained only nine compositions in Scotch; the rest of the volume was filled up with English pieces. It seems to have been only after this that Fergusson fully awoke to the great superiority of his Scotch to his English; and now little time remained to him. Growing fame led to increased conviviality. His delicate constitution was shattered by excesses, and his intellect seems to have been so far unhinged as to render him morbidly sensitive to half-accidental impressions. He had a fit of religious melancholy which affected him to the same excess as other passions, and impelled him to burn his unpublished MSS. He was beginning to recover, when an accidental fall down a staircase so injured him as to derange his mind, and make necessary his removal to the public asylum for the insane. The closing scenes are unspeakably painful. He died alone in the asylum on the 16th October, 1774, and was buried in the Canongate Churchyard.

Fergusson's poems are divided by their language into two well-marked classes, Scotch and English. The distinction, though externally one of words, goes deep. The English poems, while they are not destitute of fine touches, are as a whole of little worth. They are unreal: Sol shines in heaven, Damon and Sylvia walk the earth. A similar inferiority has been noticed in Ramsay before him and will have to be noticed, though it is less marked, in Burns after him. The reason commonly assigned is that the writers were less familiar with the English, which they only read and wrote, than with the Scotch, which they used in their daily conversation; and doubtless there is much truth in this view. But it is not the whole truth. When they attempted English, the Scottish poets were not only writing a strange language but trying to think strange thoughts as well. The English canons of taste were different from the Scotch. The poetic tradition of the Scotch impelled almost irresistibly to simplicity and truth, that of the English was such that nothing short of a revolution could suffice to shake off the trammels of convention. Thus the strange incongruity perceptible in the works of the Scottish poets may receive a perfectly natural explanation. So far as mere command of language goes, Fergusson and Ramsay were capable of writing English verse much superior to anything in that language which they have left. When they

write English however, not the language only, but sentiments and versification also are foreign to them. The
time they devote to the English muse is to these men a
species of poetic Sabbath ; for six days of their week
they "bask in Nature's smile"; on the seventh their
features must be twisted to express emotions they never
felt, and to ape graces they do not possess. And as
mere occasional imitators, who must have a precedent
for everything lest they transgress they know not what,
they are more frigid than the frigid school they followed.
In their Scotch poems, on the other hand, they are under
no such burden. Not only is the language they use
that which they had listened to and spoken from birth,
but their mental and moral atmosphere is native and
familiar. And while in their English they were hampered
with a weight of tradition far more oppressive to them
than it was to their southern brethren, in their Scotch
they were infinitely more free. This is why they
herald the return to nature before it can be said to
have begun in England, almost before any symptoms
of it can be detected. Without elaborating any theory on
the subject, and, if we exclude Burns, without anything
at all approaching Wordsworth's genius, the Scotch poets
adopt in practice much of what is best in Wordsworth's
doctrine of poetic diction and of the proper subjects for
poetic treatment.

All this is as true of Fergusson as it was of Ramsay ;
and it is this which gives to his Scotch poems that worth
and importance which his English compositions lack. In
those Scotch poems Fergusson shows that he possessed
two great gifts—the sense of humour, sometimes sarcastic

and frequently pathetic; and the sense of the beauty of nature. His humour is penetrating, but it is also kindly. In his poems on nature, which constantly recall Burns, who often imitated them, there is sometimes great sweetness; and Fergusson's feeling for nature is almost always allied with his feeling for man.

There have been considerable differences of judgment as to Fergusson's position among the poets; but on the whole the drift of critical opinion has been against him. A much lower place is commonly assigned to him now than would once have been claimed. Perhaps this is due partly to a certain impatience of the more than generous praise of Burns, who habitually speaks of Fergusson as his own equal, and sometimes as more than his equal, and who proves the sincerity of his regard by imitating Fergusson more frequently than any other poet. *The Mutual Complaint of the Plainstanes and Causey* gives the hint for *The Twa Brigs; The Farmer's Ingle* is similarly related to *The Cotter's Saturday Night*, and *Leith Races* to *The Holy Fair.* There is also kinship of spirit at least between *On Seeing a Butterfly in the Street* and Burns's *Mouse;* but in this last case there is no imitation, and probably no conscious presence of the earlier in the mind of the later poet. Burns has likewise been blamed by critics for ranking Fergusson above Ramsay: "the excellent Ramsay and the still more excellent Fergusson," are the terms in which he refers to them in his Commonplace Book. But it may be doubted whether in this particular the poet has not been a more penetrating critic than the professors of criticism. Fergusson, in his poetry as in his life, is less sane and sensible than Ramsay, in

some respects perhaps less strong; but he is infinitely
finer, he gives promise of things of which there is no
hint from beginning to end in Ramsay; and in the course
of a career which closed ere it had well begun, he displays a fervour and an elevation which the author of
The Gentle Shepherd could never rival. Ramsay was acute
and solid ; but Fergusson was a genius. It should not be
forgotten that he died at twenty-four, and that his literary
life lasted only three years. Nor is he to be contemptuously dismissed as a mere specimen of poetical precocity. In his three short years of fame he discovered where
his strength lay, learnt to distrust the questionable principles which he had been trained to respect, reversed the
proportions of his English and Scotch, and was, almost
up to the eve of his great misfortune, steadily increasing
his mastery over his native dialect. These are not the
marks of mere precocity. It is true—in the circumstances
it could not be otherwise—that his actual performance is
limited. He has left no long poem, and no proof of his
capacity to produce one. All the verse he ever wrote
can be contained within the covers of a small volume,
and only a few of his pieces are of high merit. But some
of those pieces bear the stamp of genius, immature indeed,
but real, and justify the belief that had he lived even a
few years longer his position as the inferior only of Burns
would have been beyond dispute.

Fergusson was early conscious of his gift of humour.
It is doubtful if he has left any verse earlier than his lines
on the death of Gregory ; and ill suited as the occasion was
for the display of wit, he treats even that subject in the
humorous vein. The bad taste, which would be unpardon-

able in a man, may be overlooked in the boy of fourteen.
The poet's subsequent lapse into English checked for a
while the flow of his humorous verse; for a sound instinct
taught him, as it taught nearly all his fellow poets, that
whatever the speech he might choose for his more serious
compositions, it was wisdom to express his mirth and
revelry in his native Scotch. Already however in his
earliest volume of poetry the small collection of Scotch
pieces, which were as salt to keep the whole sweet, showed
a great preponderance of the humorous element. It included, in particular, *The Daft Days*, *Braid Claith*, and
Hallowfair. From that date until his death Fergusson
continued to produce poems in a similar strain, which,
while they are frequently defaced by a coarseness that
is not so much licentious as tactless, almost always contain
evidence of rich gifts. *The Election* illustrates both the
merits and the faults of Fergusson's humour. It is needlessly coarse, in one or two passages even nauseating; but
this vice is partly redeemed by its vigour. The characters
are well outlined; the self-important deacon, the cobbler
overjoyed at the opportunity to exchange "meals o' bread
and ingans" for creams and jellies, the cooper complain-
ing of his "geyz'd" barrel, are living men. The poet's
address *To his Auld Breeks* has even greater merit without the countervailing defect. There is much fun at the
threadbare condition of bards, a touch of regret at parting
with old friends, and sly satire on the common ways of
men. *Braid Claith* likewise shows a keen appreciation
of certain weaknesses of the world with which the poor
poet had only too good reason to be acquainted. It is
much to his credit, as the piece was suggested by his own

position and experience, that there is so little bitterness
in it. He states facts without rating the world for being
what it is :—

> " Braid claith lends fouk an unco heeze,
>   Makes mony kail-worms butterflees,
>   Gies mony a doctor his degrees
>   For little skaith :
>   In short, you may be what you please
>   Wi' guid Braid Claith."

But of all Fergusson's productions in the humorous
strain the masterpiece is *Leith Races;* and it is here too
that we find the best known and perhaps the most marked
instance of contact between him and Burns. The resemblance is mainly in the introduction. In *Leith Races* the
opening stanzas run thus :—

> " In July month, ae bonny morn,
>   Whan Nature's rokelay green
>   Was spread o'er ilka rigg o' corn
>   To charm our roving een ;
>   Glowring about I saw a quean,
>   The fairest 'neath the lift ;
>   Her een were o' the siller sheen,
>   Her skin like snawy drift,
>   Sae white that day.

> " Quod she, ' I ferly unco sair,
>   That ye sud musand gae,
>   Ye wha hae sung o' Hallow-fair,
>   Her winter's pranks and play :
>   Whan on Leith-Sands the racers rare,
>   Wi' Jocky louns are met,
>   Their orrow pennies there to ware,
>   And drown themsel's in debt
>   Fu' deep that day.'

" 'And wha are ye, my winsome dear,
 That taks the gate sae early?
Whare do ye win, gin ane may spier?
 For I right meikle ferly,
That sik braw buskit laughing lass
 Thir bonny blinks shou'd gie,
An' loup like Hebe o'er the grass,
 As wanton and as free
  Frae dule this day.'

" 'I dwall amang the caller springs
 That weet the Land o' Cakes,
And aften tune my canty strings
 At bridals and late-wakes :
They ca' me Mirth ; I ne'er was kend
 To grumble or look sour,
But blythe wad be a lift to lend,
 Gif ye wad sey my pow'r
  An' pith this day.'

" 'A bargain be 't, and, by my feggs,
 Gif ye will be my mate,
Wi' you I'll screw the cherry pegs,
 Ye shanna find me blate ;
We'll reel an' ramble thro' the sands,
 And jeer wi' a' we meet ;
Nor hip the daft and gleesome bands
 That fill Edina's street
  Sae thrang this day.' "

Compare with the first stanza the opening of *The Holy
Fair* :—

" Upon a simmer Sunday morn,
 When Nature's face is fair,
I walked forth to view the corn,
 An' snuff the caller air.
The rising sun ower Galston muirs
 Wi' glorious light was glintin',
The hares were hirplin down the furs,
 The lav'rocks they were chantin'
  Fu' sweet that day."

Burns's picture is much the more poetical. Yet Fergusson's also is fine ; and in the stanzas immediately following the comparison is much less decidedly against him. It is in the satire to which these verses are introductory that the greater weight and force of the superior poet decisively tells. Fergusson is amusing, Burns incisive ; the former plays upon the surface, the latter penetrates to the core.

The poems from which these extracts have been taken, and the others to which reference has been made, relate to social life and especially to its more riotous aspects. These Fergusson was well fitted to enjoy. They appealed to the fun and frolic of his nature, to the spirit of conviviality which at once inspired him and worked his ruin. They were also the scenes amidst which the greater part of his days had been passed. All that he sings of he is familiar with. "That black banditti, the City Guard," he had known from early boyhood; and every rank of the city, from the solemn Session itself down to the street Arab, he could draw from the life. Yet it is doubtful if he was not by nature a man of the country rather than a man of the town. He viewed all country objects with keen sympathetic delight, and he painted them with skill and fidelity, in this respect far excelling Ramsay, whose references to nature are mostly incidental, and whose best services to the cause of naturalism in literature are performed in his pictures of humanity. This sense of the beauty of nature has been mentioned already as the second note of Fergusson's poetry; perhaps in point of excellence it ought to rank first; but it is not that which most readily strikes the mind of the reader. Fergusson however was too true a poet to admit of his verses being classified by the wooden divisions of "town pieces" and "country pieces," "poems of nature," and "humorous poems." Here the one note prevails, there the other; but there is often where it would be least expected—yet always naturally—a mingling of the two. He has nowhere drawn a picture of nature more finely imaginative than that which introduces *The Daft Days :—*

> "Now mirk December's dowie face
>   Glowrs owr the rigs wi' sour grimace,
>   While, thro' his *minimum* of space,
>   The blear-ey'd sun,
>   Wi' blinkin' light and stealin' pace,
>   His race doth run.
>
> "From naked groves nae birdie sings;
>   To shepherd's pipe nae hillock rings;
>   The breeze nae od'rous flavour brings
>   From Borean cave;
>   And dwyning Nature droops her wings,
>   Wi' visage grave.
>
> "Mankind but scanty pleasure glean
>   Frae snawy hill or barren plain,
>   Whan winter, 'midst his nipping train,
>   Wi' frozen spear,
>   Sends drift owr a' his bleak domain
>   And guides the weir."

As a rule Fergusson's poems on nature have reference also to man. The *Ode to the Bee* illustrates the connexion in the mind of the poet between his own race and the lower creation. The moralising is, as was almost inevitable on such a subject, somewhat hackneyed; but the conclusion, in which the Muse is likened to the bee, rises above the commonplace :—

> "Like thee, by fancy wing'd, the Muse
> Scuds ear and heartsome o'er the dews,
> Fu' vogie, and fu' blyth to crap
> The winsome flowers frae Nature's lap
> Twining her living garlands there,
> That lyart time can ne'er impair."

More characteristic are the lines *On seeing a Butterfly in the Street.* They begin by likening the insect to the human butterfly, who also seeks strange scenes to display his finery; but presently pity arises for the forlorn creature which has changed the "lintie's music" for "gruntles frae the City Guard." (Fergusson can never pass this body without a thrust more vicious than he bestows on anything else.) The poem ends with a parallel between the fate of the plain man ruined by courts and that of the luckless strayed butterfly :—

> "To sic mishanter runs the laird
> Wha quats his ha'-house an' kail-yard,
> Grows politician, scours to court,
> Whare he's the laughing-stock and sport
> Of ministers, wha jeer an' jibe,
> An' heeze his hopes wi' thought o' bribe,
> Till in the end they flae him bare,
> Leave him to poortith and to care,
> Their fleetching words o'er late he sees,
> He trudges hame, repines, and dies."

But sometimes, though rarely, and never for many successive lines, Fergusson writes without reference to man. Nowhere has he done so with more success than in the *Ode to the Gowdspink* (goldfinch), perhaps the best

of its class in the compass of his works. The praise of
the bird's beauty is worthy of the subject :—

> " Sure Nature herried mony a tree,
>   For spraings and bonny spats to thee;
>   Nae mair the rainbow can impart
>   Sic glowin' ferlies o' her art,
>   Whase pencil wrought its freaks at will
>   On thee the sey-piece o' her skill.
>   Nae mair through straths in simmer dight,
>   We seek the rose to bless our sight;
>   Or bid the bonny wa'-flowers blaw
>   Whare yonder ruins crumblin' fa':
>   Thy shining garments far outstrip
>   The cherries upo' Hebe's lip,
>   And fool the tints that Nature chose
>   To busk and paint the crimson rose."

When Burns first visited Edinburgh, finding Fergusson's
grave still unmarked, he raised a simple monument over
the remains of one with whose fate his own temperament
and his own history so well qualified him to sympathise.
The act was appropriate; for in paying respect to Fergusson the greater poet was honouring what was up to
this point the best expression of the spirit which animated
himself.

CHAPTER VIII.

THE EARLIER ANGLO-SCOTTISH SCHOOL OF THE EIGHTEENTH CENTURY.

THE proof of the assertion made in the preceding chapter, that in the eighteenth century the Scotch writers of the English language were instrumental in bringing about important changes in literature, must be found in a consideration of the men and their works. They are divisible into two groups—the first consisting of men who were born just about the opening of the century, and who flourished chiefly in the earlier half of it; the second of men some twenty or thirty years younger. The first class were the more original poets. They carried with them to England or retained in their Scottish surroundings characteristics of their own, and proved, alike by the subjects they chose, the measures they affected, and their style of treatment, that they were, if not themselves original, the scholars of masters so different from those generally followed as to give them the influence of originality.

In the earlier group are Hamilton of Bangour, Thomson, Mallet, Blair, Armstrong, and the author of Albania. They vary widely in power from Thomson, a man of unquestionable and most original genius, to Mallet, who was little better than a mere parrot; but all of them, even the weakest, brought into English literature some element which was not in it before, and which, but for the Scotch influence, either would not have appeared there or would have been later in development. It would be well to group these men together if it were only to show to what a large extent the "return to nature" towards the close of the century was influenced by Scotland. With reference to individuals, such as Thomson in his *Seasons* and Ramsay in his vernacular poems, the fact is sufficiently plain, and is readily enough acknowledged; but it is only when we gather the Scotchmen together that it becomes manifest how far their nationality was from being a mere accident, how far their ideas and tendencies were the product of their early surroundings.

Of the six men who have been mentioned, three, though born in Scotland, spent their literary life in England; of the other three, two certainly and the third probably remained in their native country. The English taste spread to Scotland and was by no means confined to those Scots who migrated to London. When Allan Ramsay began to write, the predilection of Edinburgh literary society was, as has been pointed out, all for English; and though he taught anew the relish for native verse, he never displaced the ambition to imitate and reproduce what was done in London. Among the younger wits who worked along with Ramsay, and who contributed to *The Tea Table Miscellany*, it is clear that there was as a rule a preference for English. It is a fact not without significance that in the later parts of the collection there is less and less of the Scottish tongue.

Among the contemporaries and fellow-workers of Ramsay, the most considerable was unquestionably William Hamilton of Bangour, a man sometimes but erroneously ranked with the native Scottish school. At the age of twenty he contributed to the first part of *The Tea Table Miscellany.* His life was for the most part passed un-eventfully in the best society which Edinburgh afforded, until, having involved himself in the rebellion of 1745, he had to seek safety in exile. Having been pardoned he returned in 1749; and in the following year succeeded, on the death of his elder brother, to the estate of Bangour. He died in 1754 at Lyons, whither he had gone for the sake of his health.

The most widely known of Hamilton's compositions, and on the whole the best, is the ballad of *The Braes of Yarrow*, which won from Wordsworth more admiration than it quite deserved. It professes to be written in the ancient Scottish manner; but the imitation is of the most transparent description; and it is not to be compared for depth of pathos with the best of the genuine old ballads. Hamilton has caught from them the trick of repetition; but his repetitions, which somewhat obtrusively display their purpose of heightening the effect, are quite different in spirit from the guileless yet effective repetitions of the old minstrels. The following verses present the picture which charmed Wordsworth :—

"Sweet smells the birk, green grows, green grows the grass,
  Yellow on Yarrow's braes the gowan;
 Fair hangs the apple frae the rock,
  Sweet the wave of Yarrow flowan.

 Flows Yarrow sweet, as sweet, as sweet flows Tweed,
  As green its grass, its gowan as yellow,

As sweet smells on its braes the birk,
The apple from its rock as mellow.

The secret of the enduring popularity of this ballad is its somewhat feminine sentiment and the sweetness of fancy it displays. That which delighted Wordsworth was the note of sincerity in reference to nature, a note rare enough then in England, but common to all the Scotch poets of the time. The poem is marred by that want of force which proved to be Hamilton's defect in all he ever wrote.

Among the other writings of Hamilton are included a number of translations and imitations from Homer Horace, Virgil, Anacreon, etc. Of these the only one worthy of a passing mention is a soliloquy in imitation of that of Hamlet. It is remarkable, not for its intrinsic merit, but as showing by what slight changes it is possible to pass from excellence to mediocrity. Of Hamilton's original poems, the most considerable in point of length and the most ambitious in design are *The Maid of Gallowshiels, Contemplation*, and a pair of odes *To Fancy*. The first is a fragment of an unfinished mock-heroic poem which was to have extended to twelve books, but of which only about 700 lines were written. In forming this design Hamilton had clearly mistaken the bent of his own mind. Of humour he was entirely destitute ; and without humour the mock-heroic must be a failure. The other pieces mentioned give the clue to their author's poetic descent. In an age puffed up with conceit of itself and fully assured of its superiority to all former times, he had the good taste to admire Milton and to choose him for his model. The later and

weightier works of Milton were, it is true, too lofty and
too austere for Hamilton; but his lively fancy and keen
sensibility found in the early writings of his master
something more congenial than the antithetic neatness
of Pope, something in appearance at least more approach-
able than the terse and vigorous sense of Dryden. Accordingly, though *Contemplation* is introduced with rhymed
heroics on the model of Pope, the principal part of it
is written in octosyllabic verse after the manner of Milton's *L'Allegro* and *Il Penseroso*. These poems are very
closely followed, and frequently with much skill. Hamilton's piece however is too long, and the verse has
neither the variety nor the melody of Milton's. As a
rule the reader would be inclined to credit the Scotch
poet with a sensitive ear; but there are occasional lapses
which suggest a doubt whether he had any ear at all;
and that power of fancy, which was his best gift, looks
poor beside the boundless wealth of Milton. The
following extract illustrates at once the character of
Hamilton's verse and the extent of his indebtedness :—

> "Bring Faith, endued with eagle eyes,
> That joins the earth to distant skies;
> Bland Hope that makes each sorrow less,
> Still smiling calm amid distress;
> And bring the meek-ey'd Charitie,
> Not least, tho' youngest of the three,
> Knowledge the sage, whose radiant light
> Darts quick across the mental night,
> And add warm Friendship to the train,
> Social, yielding, and humane;
> With Silence, sober-suited maid,
> Seldom on this earth survey'd :

> Bid in this sacred band appear,
> That aged venerable seer,
> With sorrowing pale, with watchings spare,
> Of pleasing yet dejected air,
> Him, heavenly Melancholy hight,
> Who flies the sons of false delight;
> Now looks serene thro' human life,
> Sees end in peace the moral strife;
> Now to the dazzling prospect blind,
> Trembles for heaven and for his kind;
> And doubting much, still hoping best,
> Late with submission finds his rest."

The criticism which applies to *Contemplation* is equally true of the two odes *To Fancy*. They follow the same model still more closely than the former; for Hamilton was one of the least original of poets. An instructive story is told with regard to some of his amatory poetry. The lady who was its subject, rather annoyed than flattered by its warmth, consulted a friend how she might best protect herself from such unwelcome attentions. He sagaciously advised her to make a pretence of taking the verses seriously and accepting the advances; whereupon the alarmed poet became cold and distant. So it is too frequently with Hamilton's poetry. Like many another versifier, he took up a subject rather because he thought he could write prettily than because he felt deeply upon it. Though, therefore, in an age when tastes so different from Milton's were almost universally diffused, it is interesting to listen to an echo of his voice, however weak, yet clearly little was to be expected from a poet so essentially imitative. Hamilton's vein, though it yielded a little fair-seeming ore, was far from rich. All that can be justly claimed for him is that he did something to

divert taste towards earlier and greater models than those
of his own age, and that he struck a note or two, hardly
more, in the natural key.

His contemporary, James Thomson, was a man of very
different stamp and of far higher rank in literature. It
was he who, more than any other individual in the first
three-quarters of the eighteenth century, taught England
the fallacy of the current canons of taste and criticism.
He was born in 1700, at Ednam, in Roxburghshire,
where his father was minister.   While he was still a boy
he was "discovered" by Robert Riccaltoun, then a
farmer, afterwards minister of Hobkirk, who encouraged
and drew out the talent he perceived in young Thomson.
After spending a few years at the grammar school of
Jedburgh, the boy was sent in 1715 to the University
of Edinburgh, where it was intended that he should
study for the ministry.   In 1716, only a few months
after he had begun his college career, his father died
under circumstances so peculiar, and so vividly illustrative of the spirit of the time, that they deserve to be re-
counted.   His parish—not Ednam, but Southdean, near
Jedburgh, to which he had removed in the year of the
poet's birth—was troubled with a ghost; and the minister
was required to exorcise it.   He was on this point no
more enlightened than his congregation, and was in the
act of performing the ceremony of exorcism when he was
seized with a sudden and rapidly fatal illness.   The
story ran that he was struck with a ball of fire.   His
fate made a deep impression on his son's nerves; and
Mr. J. Logie Robertson is probably right in connecting
with it that sense of the supernatural, bordering on

superstition, which several times finds expression in Thomson's poetry.

The death of her husband induced Mrs. Thomson to remove to Edinburgh, where, as she had been heiress to a small fortune, she was still able, with economy, to defray the expenses of her son's education. But though his connexion with the University continued till 1724, he never entered the profession for which he had been destined. He showed a constantly growing predilection for poetry. He had been from an early age a scribbler of verse, but had sufficient power of self-criticism to destroy his own boyish productions. It does not appear that he printed any specimens of his poetry prior to the publication in 1720 of some of his pieces in *The Edinburgh Miscellany*, a collection issued by the Athenian Society, one of the numerous literary clubs of the Scottish capital. Thomson's contributions were of no permanent value; but one of them, *On a Country Life*, has been thought to contain the germ of *The Seasons*. Though a crude and boyish piece, it has the merit of being the outcome of real observation of nature, and it proves Thomson to have been already, so far, free from the fetters of the artificial school. There is in it much the same range of topics that we afterwards find in the more elaborate work—a few hints about each of the seasons, something relating to country sports, etc. The aspiration after a country life with which it concludes expresses Thomson's lifelong preference, a preference which explains his choice of subjects. The verse is the heroic couplet, which was at this time Thomson's favourite measure; but both the lines *On a Country*

Life and the other pieces where he employs it are harsh and unpolished.

In 1725 Thomson, having determined to abandon the Church, and apparently to enter upon a career of letters, turned his steps towards London. Whether he had any other employment in view is uncertain. His vague hints to his friends certainly suggest some more definite occupation than that of a writer of verses; but his hopes, if he really entertained any, were disappointed. It is pleasing to notice that his first regular employment was due to the influence of Lady Grizzel Baillie, herself a poetess, though she too rarely exerted her talent. Through her he became tutor in the family of her son-in-law, Lord Binning. But he soon gave up this post, and occupied himself with his *Winter*, which at first consisted merely of detached poetical notes on that season. It was published in 1726 by a bookseller who bought it for three guineas. *Summer* followed in 1727, *Spring* in 1728, and *Autumn*, completing the cycle, in 1730. Thomson's poetry had been successful almost from the first; and by the time *The Seasons* was finished he was one of the most celebrated men of letters in England. He had made little money by his verses, but he had formed connexions from which he might fairly hope for much in the future.

Thomson well deserved all the fame he won from *The Seasons*. It is the most original contribution to English poetry in the long interval between the death of Dryden, perhaps even between the death of Milton, and the rise of the Revolutionary school. There are in that period some works which must rank above Thomson's in other respects; but there is none which is so much the product of one mind. Johnson long ago noted this originality as Thomson's highest claim to praise; but he was himself too much imbued with the prevailing spirit of his time to discover its peculiar value. It is not merely that Thomson had a style of his own and a versification of his own; nor even is the matter ended when it has been said that his choice of a subject of itself marked him out from the common herd of versifiers. This is essentially true; and yet Thomson's originality is thrown into all the stronger relief by the fact that most of his contemporaries coquetted with rural subjects. Though Pope, Philips, Gay, and Parnell had all tried such themes, it remained possible for Wordsworth to assert that "excepting the *Nocturnal Reverie* of Lady Winchilsea, and a passage or two in the *Windsor Forest* of Pope, the poetry of the period intervening between the publication of the *Paradise Lost* and the *Seasons* does not contain a single new image of external nature." It would be dangerous to affirm the literal truth of this criticism. Thomson's countryman, Ramsay, certainly wrote with his eye on nature, and English poetry too was somewhat less barren than Wordsworth imagined; yet its substantial justice is generally admitted. The period of which Wordsworth writes was in the first place one which exalted the town far above the country: its spirit is expressed in Johnson's well-known preference for Fleet Street above all other scenes on earth. The organisation of literary society tended to give additional strength to this preference. The poets herded together almost of necessity in the London clubs. It is hardly conceivable therefore that they should be original in their pictures of external nature.   But further, it is well known that the ambition of the age did not aim at originality of matter at all.   The poetical chief of the time, Pope, held and avowed the belief that all ideas had been exhausted by former poets, and that for his own age it only remained to clothe those ideas in a more becoming garb.   And in this faith and this practice the whole host of minor poets followed him.   If therefore they stumbled upon an original idea at all, it was by accident ; they certainly could not consistently with their theory seek it.

It is easy to see why such a theory obtained currency. There is plausibility in the view that the ceaseless toil of generation after generation of keen and eager minds must at length exhaust the matter for thought, at least in some departments.   A long succession of poets, from Homer down, had been occupied in saying the best things about nature, about human society, about the future destiny of man ; what, it was argued, could remain for the modern to add ?   The same line of argument, it is true, might have been applied with even greater plausibility to style. If the labour of centuries must have used up the matter of poetry, much more was it likely to have exhausted all possible varieties of manner ; for in style the scope is far more limited.   But had the argument been pushed so far the poet's occupation would have been gone ; and the authors of it wisely stopped short of the point of annihilation.   The spirit which thus found its expression is by no means confined to the age of Pope.   It is at the root of the cheap cynicism of the present day, which tells us that there is no such thing as originality outside the walls of a lunatic asylum, the one place probably where originality is never found. The refutation is not difficult. It may proceed either by the argument *a priori* or *a posteriori*. On the former line it will be sufficient to suggest that whatever verbal definition of poetry we may accept, it will always be found to signify that poetry is the expression of some kind of thought and is somehow related to human life. But thought according to the philosophers is infinite; and human life both philosophers and biologists are agreed in describing as a constant series of changes, related to but always different from the past. The error then of the Queen Anne poets is cognate to the exploded doctrine that there is a cycle in human affairs, and that after a certain lapse of ages variety is exhausted and things repeat themselves. We know, on the contrary, that the wheel never comes full circle, or more properly, that there is no wheel at all to complete its circle. The course of human affairs may possibly be represented by a spiral curve, but not by a curve which returns upon itself.

If the fallacy be attacked from the side of experience, the conclusion is the same; and it carries to the English mind an authority which abstract argument never bears. Is it true in point of fact that the earlier poets are more original than the later ones? In such an inquiry it is obviously unfair to go back to the point at which our information ends; because there we have no means of determining the extent of the indebtedness to predecessors who remain unknown. It is impossible to estimate the indebtedness of Homer, because it is impossible to discover who were the poets before him. If therefore we take the penultimate stage, we find the same sort of indebtedness to predecessors then as now. Was Chaucer more original than Browning? No competent judge will doubt that the balance inclines quite the other way. Milton inherited many ages of literature after Virgil. Was he therefore less original? Both owed much to predecessors : he who will may weigh and measure their exact indebtedness. Wherever the light of history is tolerably full and clear, we find that the degree of originality is much the same from age to age; where it is dim and doubtful, originality appears greatest on the side on which knowledge is most limited. One man will always differ from another in power of origination; but the possibilities open are much the same in all ages of history. Robert Browning, one of the latest of the world's great poets, is also one of the most independent.

These reflections are so obvious that they would be scarcely worth expressing were it not clear that they are often missed even now, and that in the period under investigation most men were entirely blind to them—so blind that it needed an original genius to combat in practice the opposite belief. This was what Thomson did; and to have done it successfully is his peculiar glory. Refusing to believe that all the truth about nature, that is, all the poetic truth, was to be found in books, all that was worth learning to be learnt in towns, he looked with his own eyes, listened with his own ears, pondered in his own heart upon what he saw and heard, and, as the result, added more of the freshness of nature to English verse than all his predecessors from Dryden downward. How far he was inspired to do this by the place of his nativity and his early training, it would be interesting to learn more fully and conclusively than it is possible to discover from the known facts of his life. He has however recorded his obligation to a minor poet of his native district for the idea of *The Seasons.* It was suggested to his mind by a poem of his early friend, Robert Riccaltoun, on *Winter.* It is also said that much of the scenery of *The Seasons* is drawn from the vale of Jed.[1] Further, it is to be noted that Thomson was born and bred in the midst of that district where tradition still preserved those fine old ballads which Scott afterwards gathered together in *The Minstrelsy of the Scottish Border.* Though the style of them cannot be traced in Thomson, it seems more than probable that they gave him or confirmed in him, perhaps unconsciously, a taste which he never lost. He could not be ignorant of them; and the single piece in the Scottish dialect which he has left, the *Elegy on James Thorburn,* is remarkable at least as a proof of his acquaintance with one of the most distinctive of Scottish stanzas.

But, though Thomson was eminently original, he shared, as was inevitable, many of the tendencies of his time. It is easy to detect in his rich and rather too profusely ornate style something of that inflation which is so prominent in Johnson, the incarnation of the spirit of his age. Thomson has no conception of the power of a severe simplicity; and though the sincerity of his thought redeems him, yet the reader often feels that his language is unnecessarily florid and luxuriant. Frequently he sinks to the worst affectations of "poetic diction." Sheep are "the bleating kind," birds "the feathered people" or

[1] Mr. Logie Robertson's edition of Thomson, p. 3.

"the plumy nation," eggs "ovarious food," rustics "the fond sequacious herd." But if such phrases be taken to represent the Tartarean depth to which Thomson is capable of sinking, they may be balanced with others which show his head reared as high towards heaven; for though his characteristic in *The Seasons* is rather level excellence throughout than extraordinary beauty in detached lines and phrases, he does, like almost all true poets, afford such lines, a few of which have stamped themselves upon the popular memory. The world will not readily forget

> "On utmost Kilda's shore, whose lonely race
> Resign the setting sun to Indian worlds,"

or the kindred picture of the region

> "Where the Northern Ocean in vast whirls
> Boils round the naked melancholy isles
> Of farthest Thule, and the Atlantic surge
> Pours in among the stormy Hebrides."

They have a taste of Thomson's habitual gorgeousness, but only such as the thought demands. There is a charm too in the allusion to Hampden,

> "Who stemmed the torrent of a downward age
> To slavery prone";

and in the reference to Drake with its grandly sonorous close,

> "A Drake who made thee mistress of the deep,
> And bore thy name in thunder round the world."

Time has proved also the happiness of the description of that loveliness which "is when unadorned adorned the most," and of the lover who "sighed and looked unutterable things."

Most of these examples are on subjects which Thomson did not make peculiarly his own. From his own proper sphere may be gathered still finer specimens of his art. It would be difficult to surpass the line in which he describes the verdure and the unnumbered flowers of the meadow as "the negligence of nature, wide and wild"; and Mr. Saintsbury has justly praised the picture of "the yellow wallflower stained with iron-brown" as perfect of its kind. In another style, but scarcely less admirable, is the description of a swollen winter stream :—

"It boils, and wheels, and foams, and thunders through."

The line not only raises up before the eye a picture of the furious torrent, but fills the ear with its roar. Again, for concise truth and rich suggestiveness the following lines will bear comparison with almost any :—

"The plaint of rills,
That, purling down amid the twisted roots
Which creep around, their dewy murmurs shake
On the soothed ear."

Here every epithet is pictorial, and not a word can be spared without damage to the whole. The same merits are seen in the lines descriptive of the appearance of the sky at the beginning of a winter storm :—

"Rising slow,
Blank in the leaden-coloured east, the moon
Wears a wan circle round her blunted horns."

Sometimes a single epithet is enough to betray the master hand, as in the picture of the bird not to be tempted from her nest, "though the whole *loosened* Spring

around her blow "; or in the adjective which he applies
to a summer night, " With quickened step *Brown* night
retires," where the ' brown ' is felt to be as true as it is
novel.

It will be observed that the best of these quotations
are as simple as the thought will permit them to be.
There are however few continuous passages of many
lines in Thomson of which this can be said. He had
a taste for rotundity of phrase, for ear-filling words. This
fault is conspicuous in the luscious description of the
glories of the torrid zone which, with kindred themes,
fills a great part of *Summer* — the longest, and on
the whole the weakest, of the four poems which make
up *The Seasons*. There is however visible also in those
passages that striving after truth which would have redeemed more serious errors. Thomson had never been
in tropical climates, and it was inevitable that there
should be less of reality in his description of them than
in passages depicting scenes with which his daily walks
had rendered him familiar. But he had read carefully
to prepare himself by the best means in his power for
his task, and he made a strenuous effort to reconstruct a
real scene. He is partly, but not completely, successful.
On the one hand he escapes the common fallacy of
describing the tropics as rich in many-coloured flowers ;
on the other he makes the hippopotamus walk the plains
and seek the hills for food.

This determination to be faithful is the ruling spirit of
The Seasons. It carried Thomson much farther than the
casual reader is apt to see. He was not content with
the external appearance of things, but always sought to

penetrate beneath the surface; and if it is a merit in the painter to study anatomy that he may the better understand the true play of human muscles, surely it is no less a merit of the poet to make himself acquainted with botany that his descriptions may be the more true and exact. Such knowledge may doubtless be perverted, as it was by the sculptor who has left that monstrosity of Milan Cathedral, a human figure stripped of its skin; or as it was in Erasmus Darwin's *Botanic Garden.* Examples may be found in Thomson himself of a not very poetical use of knowledge; but as in the main he is free from pedantry, the trouble he took to extend his information must be ranked on virtue's side. The only matter for regret is that it was not sufficient to preserve him entirely from mistakes.

But, apart from the question of the more than ample compensations which Thomson affords, it is impossible altogether to regret the splendour of taste which results in verse such as this, in which the poet connects the radiance of gems with the sunlight :—

> "At thee the ruby lights its deepening glow,
> And with a waving radiance inward flames;
> From thee the sapphire, solid ether, takes
> Its hue cerulean; and, of evening tinct,
> The purple-streaming amethyst is thine.
> With thy own smile the yellow topaz burns;
> Nor deeper verdure dyes the robe of Spring,
> When first she gives it to the southern gale,
> Than the green emerald shows. But, all combined,
> Thick through the whitening opal play thy beams;
> Or, flying several from its surface, form
> A trembling variance of revolving lines,
> As the site varies in the gazer's hand."

Another extract will illustrate Thomson's more sober-hued style :—

> "Now from the town,
> Buried in smoke, and deep, and noisome damps,
> Oft let me wander o'er the dewy fields,
> Where freshness breathes, and dash the trembling drops
> From the bent bush, as through the verdant maze
> Of sweet-briar hedges I pursue my walk ;
> Or taste the smell of dairy ; or ascend
> Some eminence, Augusta, of thy plains,
> And see the country, far diffused around,
> One boundless blush, one white empurpled shower
> Of mingled blossoms : where the raptured eye
> Hurries from joy to joy ; and, hid beneath
> In fair profusion, yellow Autumn smiles."

It is to be regretted that this passage is marred by the affected name, Augusta, for London ; but except for that there is nothing which could be wished away. The style is perfectly simple where simplicity is desirable, and warms and colours when the subject demands it.

To the poetry of which these extracts are specimens—favourable specimens, no doubt—a very high rank must be assigned. It is in the first place absolutely true. Those conventionalities which suggest that Thomson is not genuine to the core are mere excrescences upon his style, the bad inheritance of his age. And secondly, the truth which he gives the world is new. The thought is his own, and equally his own is the versification. He rejects the favourite metre of the day for blank verse ; and though in particular phrases and turns of expression the reader may detect the influence which Milton must always exercise over anyone who adopts his measure, Thomson's verse is no mere echo of that of any earlier poet. Johnson justly remarks, " His numbers, his pauses, his diction, are of his own growth, without transcription, without imitation."

Even in *The Seasons* however there are evidences of the limitations which prevented Thomson from fulfilling those higher hopes which an early work of such distinguished merit inevitably inspired. One such indication is the frequent recurrence of identical rhythms. Another, which goes deeper, is an insufficiency, under all its gorgeousness, in Thomson's diction. His eye saw more than his pen could express. Thus :—

> " How clear the cloudless sky ! how deeply tinged
> With a *peculiar* blue."

The poet sees that the blue requires an adjective to define it, but that which he supplies is not pictorial.

A noticeable feature of Thomson is the almost complete absence from his poetry of that "pathetic fallacy" which, by identifying the feelings of man with the spirit of nature, has, to the modern mind, given so deep a charm to much of our later verse. This "pathetic fallacy" made its appearance soon after Thomson. It is present in the poetry of Fergusson; it tinges still more deeply that of Burns; and it is of the very essence of Wordsworth's. But in Thomson there is very little of it. Even a passing touch, such as "the plaint of rills" in one of the passages quoted above, is exceptional. He was not an idealist; he sought simply to depict what he saw, and what apparently everyone might easily see. On the other hand, if Thomson was a realist, he was assuredly not one of the type to which the garbage of nature is as valuable and as well worthy

of description as her noblest scenes. He discriminated.
The most commonplace scene was good enough for his
verse provided it was perfect of its kind; but decay and
dissolution were, to him, matter for reference, not for
elaborate portraiture.

Thomson's successors felt his power, his truth, and his
deep originality. Wordsworth looked back to him as an
early champion of a reviving natural school, and sometimes imitated him. In the *Highland Girl* the lines,

> "Twice seven consenting years have shed
> Their utmost bounty on thy head,"

are plainly suggested by Thomson :—

> "Consenting Spring
> Sheds her own rosy garland on their heads."

Coleridge studied him. A few lines of Thomson call
to mind the magnificent melodies of the *Hymn before
Sunrise in the Vale of Chamouni*, and are not unworthy
of comparison even with that masterpiece :—

> "Meantime, amid these upper seas, condensed
> Around the cold aereal mountain's brow,
> And by conflicting winds together dashed,
> The thunder holds his black tremendous throne."

And the following extract from the grand hymn which
closes *The Seasons* will prove that the still grander hymn
of Coleridge owed more to Thomson than a mere chance
cadence or expression. The elder poet, it is true, does
not equal one of the most gifted minds in the rolls of
English poetry in one of its loftiest flights; and it would
be a poor spirit which would grudge to Coleridge the

suggestions he has known so well how to improve upon. But the parallel is worthy of attention :—

> "To Him, ye vocal gales,
> Breathe soft, whose Spirit in your freshness breathes ;
> Oh talk of Him in solitary glooms
> Where, o'er the rock, the scarcely waving pine
> Fills the brown shade with a religious awe.
> And ye, whose bolder note is heard afar,
> Who shake the astonished world, lift high to heaven
> The impetuous song, and say from whom you rage.
> His praise, ye brooks, attune, ye trembling rills,
> And let me catch it as I muse along.
> Ye headlong torrents, rapid and profound ;
> Ye softer floods, that lead the humid maze
> Along the vale ; and thou, majestic main,
> A secret world of wonders in thyself,
> Sound His stupendous praise whose greater voice
> Or bids you roar, or bids your roarings fall."

Nothing has as yet been said, and little need be said, of the plan of *The Seasons*. The poem cannot with much meaning be said to have a plan. Thomson himself began with *Winter*, and it is a matter almost of indifference how the parts are arranged. That we regard spring as the beginning of a cycle of changes which ends in the death of winter is indeed a reason for the order of the four poems ; but the question why the pictures in each are just such and not something different is one to which no satisfactory answer can be given. That the poet was sensible of this is proved by the fact that in editions after the first—for he was constantly altering, polishing, adding, and transposing—some passages are even removed from one season to another. This want of vital unity is doubtless a defect of the poem, and is probably the chief reason why, although it is recognised by all who read it as a great work, *The Seasons* no longer enjoys the full measure of popularity which is due to its merits, and which not so very long ago it still retained. But the difficulty was insuperable. If such a work was to be written at all, it could not, as regards plan, be done better than Thomson did it.

A success so decided as that achieved by *The Seasons* naturally encouraged its author to further poetic ventures. Even before it was finished, in 1729, he published another poem entitled *Britannia*, which enjoyed a fleeting popularity and was afterwards not undeservedly forgotten. Thomson, though a fervid patriot, was unfortunate in his attempts to wed patriotism to verse. His song, *Rule, Britannia*, which first appeared in the masque of *Alfred*, the joint work of Thomson and Mallet, is only too well known for his poetic fame; and another more ambitious but even less successful effort must shortly be noticed. His first play, *Sophonisba*, followed in 1730. It enjoyed a qualified and brief success, due rather to the reputation won by *The Seasons* than to its own merits. Thomson however had a love for the theatre, and over and over again tried his fortune in dramatic composition. *Agamemnon* was put upon the stage in 1738. Another tragedy, *Edward and Eleanora*, was ready for representation the following year; but on political grounds the necessary license was refused. *Tancred and Sigismunda* followed in 1745; and finally the posthumous play of *Coriolanus* in 1749. It can only be matter for regret that Thomson wasted so much of his life over compositions in which he was so little qualified to excel. He had not the dramatic faculty. His plays are cold, lifeless, and uninteresting. They are equal in bulk to all his other poetry combined, yet there is hardly a line in the whole for the loss of which the world would be poorer.

The five years which had passed between the arrival of Thomson in London and the completion of *The Seasons* had raised him to the first rank of literary fame. It seemed as if he was now about to reap the material fruits of his success. In 1730 he was asked to accompany Charles Talbot, eldest son of Sir Charles Talbot, who subsequently became Lord Chancellor, as travelling companion through France and Italy. The office not only afforded him present support and the prospect of future preferment, but promised a widening of his education and experiences which might well be expected to enrich his poetry. On his return, after an absence of more than a year, he began to work on the poem which was afterwards published under the title of *Liberty*. Young Talbot was dead before its completion, and it was dedicated to his memory by the grateful Thomson, who owed to the patronage of the father the office of Secretary of Briefs in Chancery.

Liberty is a long poem in five parts, published in sections in three successive years, 1734, 1735, and 1736. It is as a whole dull, and except in a few passages shows little of the beauty of *The Seasons*. It is bad in design; and nothing but superlative excellence of style could on such a subject atone for ignorance of history and a false political philosophy. The poem, which is a vision wherein the Goddess of Liberty traces her own career, begins in the middle with a comparison between

the ancient and modern state of Italy; works backward
to the first rise of liberty and its transmission down to
Greece; goes on to its rise, progress, and decline in
Rome; its retirement from earth in the dark ages; its
reappearance in Britain; and ends with a vision of the
future. The whole is heavy and laboured, confused, and
often pompous. The beauties are like Gratiano's reasons,
hid in too much chaff to be worth the search.

In 1736 Thomson, by this time a tolerably prosperous
man, removed to Richmond, where he could indulge his
special tastes better than in London; but the death of
Lord Talbot in the following year, depriving him of his
office, reduced him again to poverty. He was soon
however relieved from his more pressing wants by a
pension of £100 from the Prince of Wales, to whom in
gratitude he dedicated his play of *Agamemnon.* In 1744
he was appointed, through the influence of Lord Lyttelton,
Surveyor-General of the Leeward Islands, a post which,
after paying his deputy, brought him £300 a year. In
1748 *The Castle of Indolence* was published. Some three
months later in the same year the poet died of a chill
caught on the river. He was attended on his death-bed
by his fellow-countryman and fellow-poet, Dr. Armstrong.

The Castle of Indolence, the triumph which signalised
the close of Thomson's career as *The Seasons* marked
its beginning, was a work on which he had laboured
lovingly for nearly fifteen years, enlarging, touching, and
refining. As was the case with *The Seasons* too, the
plan of it grew under his hand. He began merely with the
intention of writing a few stanzas in order to turn back upon
his friends the charge of idleness which they were accus-

tomed to prefer against him. The subject proved congenial, and the few stanzas grew into a poem of two cantos, one of the most highly finished and one of the most imaginative of the productions of the eighteenth century. It is written in the stanza of Spenser, whose manner is imitated and whose languorous charm of style has been caught to an astonishing degree. And yet *The Castle of Indolence* is very much more than an imitation; indeed, when viewed in reference to the age in which it was written, it is scarcely less original than *The Seasons* itself. We might suppose that Thomson had set himself to teach his time two lessons, and had embodied those lessons in two poems. The first was the lesson that careful observation and fidelity to fact would still repay the poet; the second, not less surprising to a rationalising age, was that human nature possessed a faculty beyond the understanding, and was not to be satisfied by an appeal to that alone. It has been already remarked that in *The Seasons* Thomson is realistic in the sense that he paints what he actually sees,—imaginatively, yet still in such a way that even a prosaic mind may follow him and understand him. There is no Turneresque light upon his landscape to repel one type of mind as violently as it attracts another. In *The Castle of Indolence* he writes as an idealist for idealists; and though a little reflection detects the same nature beneath both, it seems at first sight as if the two poems were the product of different minds. In both cases we see a man whose interest in society is altogether subordinate to his interest in the phenomena of his own mind. These phenomena may be regarded either from the external or from the internal point of view; and Thomson has taken each in turn. In *The Seasons* there is little direct yet there is a constant indirect subjective reference. The one point of union between the various pictures is that they are the perceptions of the poet's mind. He speaks to his brother men, but to them only through his own personal experience. In *The Castle of Indolence* we look inward; but there is no other essential change. We still find Thomson teaching through the medium, not of what he had gathered to be the experience of other men, but of what he knew as his own. And the atmosphere of the two poems differs only as the difference of subject suggested. There is an elusive vagueness in the phenomena of the inner world which contrasts with the definiteness and solidity, as it appears at least, of the outer world, much as the delicate beauty of *The Castle of Indolence* contrasts with the more solid and palpable excellence of *The Seasons*.

The first canto of *The Castle of Indolence* is devoted to a description of the enchanter's castle, his allurements, the inhabitants of his domain, and their mode of life. The whole is drawn by a master hand. Few things in poetry are more beautiful or more admirably fitted to the purpose than the opening description of the castle. Thomson has anticipated in it Tennyson's conception of the "land where it was always afternoon." The two poets worked independently, and both exquisitely.

> "In lowly dale, fast by a river's side,
>   With woody hill o'er hill encompass'd round,
> A most enchanting wizard did abide,
>   Than whom a fiend more fell is nowhere found.
>   It was, I ween, a lovely spot of ground;

And there a season atween June and May,
 Half prankt with spring, with summer half imbrown'd,
A listless climate made, where, sooth to say,
No living wight could work, ne cared ev'n for play.

" Was nought around but images of rest :
 Sleep-soothing groves, and quiet lawns between ;
And flowery beds that slumberous influence kest,
 From poppies breath'd ; and beds of pleasant green,
 Where never yet was creeping creature seen.
Meantime unnumber'd glittering streamlets play'd,
 And hurl'd everywhere their waters sheen ;
That, as they bicker'd through the sunny glade,
Though restless still themselves a lulling murmur made.

" Join'd to the prattle of the purling rills,
 Were heard the lowing herds along the vale,
And flocks loud-bleating from the distant hills,
 And vacant shepherds piping in the dale :
 And now and then sweet Philomel would wail,
Or stock-doves plain amid the forest deep,
 That drowsy rustled to the sighing gale ;
And still a coil the grasshopper did keep ;
Yet all these sounds yblent inclined all to sleep.

" Full in the passage of the vale, above,
 A sable, silent, solemn forest stood ;
Where nought but shadowy forms was seen to move,
 As Idless fancied in her dreaming mood :
 And up the hills, on either side, a wood
Of blackening pines, ay waving to and fro,
 Sent forth a sleepy horror through the blood ;
And where this valley winded out, below,
The murmuring main was heard, and scarcely heard, to
 flow.

" A pleasing land of drowsihead it was,
 Of dreams that wave before the half-shut eye ;
And of gay castles in the clouds that pass,
 For ever flushing round a summer sky :
 There eke the soft delights, that witchingly

> Instil a wanton sweetness through the breast,
>   And the calm pleasures always hover'd nigh:
> But whate'er smack'd of noyance, or unrest,
> Was far far off expelled from this delicious nest."

The wizard who dwells in this enchanted ground is master of a song not unworthy of it. By the example of the butterfly in prime of May, and of the birds which neither plough nor sow, yet enjoy the harvest, he calls upon man, the outcast of nature, to lay down his load of care and enjoy ease unbroken or varied only by that gentle exercise which is a pleasure. This wizard, his porter, whose " calm, broad, thoughtless aspect breath'd repose," and the porter's page, careless of all but sleep and play, are the rulers of the scene. They take the victims drawn by the alluring song within their domain, give them draughts from the fountain of Nepenthe, and proclaim to them that all are at liberty to follow their own pleasure. Whereupon, so innumerable are the paths of desire, the multitude vanish,

> "As when a shepherd of the Hebrid-isles,
>   Plac'd far amid the melancholy main,
> (Whether it be lone fancy him beguiles;
>   Or that aerial beings sometimes deign
>   To stand embodied, to our senses plain)
> Sees on the naked hill, or valley low,
>   The whilst in ocean Phoebus dips his wain,
> A vast assembly moving to and fro:
> Then all at once in air dissolves the wondrous show."

All that can soothe the sense or charm the taste, every delicacy of food and drink, every pleasing colour and form and sound, enrich and adorn those courts and halls. These delights are sketched with great skill, though

Thomson checks himself in the middle and declares that his muse has no colours which can glow like that fairy-land. Portraits are added of a few of the inhabitants of the place, including the poet himself, "more fat than bard beseems," but "void of envy, guile, and lust of gain." The canto ends significantly with a picture of a place discovered too late, a place

> " Deep, dreary, underground,
> Where still our inmates, when unpleasing grown,
> Diseas'd, and loathsome, privily were thrown."

The second canto displays the other side of the picture. It tells the story of the birth and nurture of Sir Industry, his progress over the world till he settles in Britain, and his final retirement there to pass the evening of his days in a well-earned repose. But the news that Indolence is eating away the morals of the land and ruining the works which he had reared rouses Sir Industry. He sallies out attended by his bard Philo-melus, and seeks the Castle. Even these champions of toil feel the charm of the enchanter's art ; but the Knight subdues him and then calls upon the Bard to rouse with his song the souls of those who are not altogether lost. He responds with a fine strain which is meant to contrast with that of Indolence in the first canto, and with the picture of his slumberous land. The essence of it is that action is always preferable to inactivity, as the stream is preferable to the stagnant pool. The better sort rise to his appeal, but the greater part curse both Bard and Knight as sons of hate disturbing the seat of peace and love. The Knight then waves a wand which dispels the enchantment and shows the inhabitants the native

hideousness of the place.   He promises help to all who
will repent.   The impenitent must suffer deeply before
their stains are wept away; but even for them Thomson's
kindly philosophy has hope:—

> "Who can say
> What grace may yet shine forth in heaven's eternal day?"

The poem ends with a description of the misery of those
who will not be rescued.

The same fate which has in art so often exalted the
picture of evil above that of good, which has awarded
the palm to Dante's *Inferno* in preference to his *Paradiso,*
to Milton's hell rather than his heaven, has decreed
that Thomson's delineation of Indolence should excel
that of Industry.   The second canto is good, but there
is nothing in it which for poetic beauty can be compared
with the best passages of the first; nor is the impression
of the whole nearly so pleasing.   There may be some
common cause which has helped to bring about the like
result in all these cases; but there was also a special
cause at work in Thomson's case.   He loved ease, and
his Castle of Indolence is drawn by one who had felt
all the delights of which he writes.

One of the highest qualities of the poem is the delicacy
with which the moral of it is woven in with the artistic
fabric.   To accomplish this union satisfactorily is always
one of the most difficult tasks that can be set the poet;
and it was one in which Thomson's contemporaries were
rarely successful.   But he possessed the skill which they
lacked.   Without shutting from view one delight which
Indolence can claim as his own, without ignoring the
possibility of combining indolence with action, provided

the action be unencumbered with a purpose, without even denying the tincture of virtue there is in vice itself, he yet succeeds in presenting the loathsome den which ultimately engulfs the idle as the natural goal of their life, and this in a manner quite unobtrusive. And the contrasting figure of Industry is drawn, if not with equal charm, at least with convincing force. The moral is that they who live the life of butterflies must accept the fate of the butterfly, must be content to be the sport of circumstances; while they who with their own right hand are architects of their own fortune will naturally enjoy whatever of beautiful or of good their labour has created.

The patience with which Thomson endeavoured to perfect his poem was well bestowed. *The Castle of Indolence*, though less important in the history of poetry, is in some respects preferable even to *The Seasons*. Though it was a casual growth it cannot be charged with that defect of plan which betrays itself in the earlier poem. There is a natural sequence of the ideas, a natural development of the thought, the parts are linked each to each by natural harmony. The style is, if not better, at any rate finer and more delicate. Objections may be taken by some to the archaisms in imitation of Spenser; but most readers will probably think that the Spenserian stanza has become so associated in tradition with archaic forms as almost to demand them before it will yield its full flavour.

One of the most peculiar points in the history of Thomson is that he should twice and no oftener have achieved such distinguished success. In virtue of either *The Seasons* or *The Castle of Indolence*, still more of both, most critics would be willing to grant him a place among the minor giants, not the gods, of poetry; some would be inclined, on a review of his work in connexion with the time and circumstances in which it was produced, to make that place far from a low one. Those two poems are unmistakeably the work of a man of genius. Yet in all else that he wrote, considerable as it is in quantity and varied as it is in character, the reader seldom even for a moment, and never for many consecutive lines, feels that he is in the presence of a great man. The songs to Amanda, though inspired by a real passion, are at the best of only moderate merit. The miscellaneous songs have even less to recommend them. About the tragedies, *Liberty* and *Britannia*, the world has long ago made up its mind. Among the minor poems which have not been noticed there is little that would attract even a passing glance but for the name of Thomson. The best of them, the *Hymn on Solitude*, does contain a few lines in his happiest manner; but exceptional passages such as this are not sufficient to disturb the general judgment that Thomson is memorable for *The Seasons* and *The Castle of Indolence* alone. He stumbled upon the one subject at the very opening of his career, the other he had not finished till he was almost on the verge of the grave. Whether, if length of days had been granted him, he would have written more that the world would not willingly let die, or whether he would have groped blindly on from blunder to blunder as he did through so many of the years that were actually his, can never be determined. Thus much is certain, that his inspiration ·was not at his own command; that he had no canon of self-criticism by which he could discriminate between what was possible for him and what was impossible; that the worth of his work was wholly dependent upon a felicitous choice of subject; and that according as the subject suited or did not suit him, he displayed the head of gold or the feet of clay. To define what suited him is not easy. He made no approach to definition himself; but at least a little may be done by negatives. Nothing suited him which demanded, like the drama, the mergence of self in the character of another; nothing which, like *Liberty*, demanded a combination of history and philosophy; nothing which, like the songs, called for the concentrated expression of intense passion. Byron detected that Thomson was weak on the subject of love. The episodes in *The Seasons*, if they may be so called, are feeble; and what is worse, they betray a strain of coarseness in the poet's mind. His genius was reflective rather than passionate; and self, in no offensive sense, was always the pivot of his reflection.

Thomson, though he was not the founder of a school, exercised a well marked influence over the poets of his time. He was the first after Milton who for non-dramatic purposes employed blank verse on a large scale; and all the very considerable body of eighteenth century verse in that measure must be regarded as, in greater or less degree, due to his example. But he was especially influential over his own countrymen; and of these no one followed him more closely than David Mallet. Mallet, who had studied at Edinburgh in the same years with Thomson, preceded him to London, and was one of the first to reach him a helping hand there.   His fidelity to his fellow student, for which Thomson was lastingly grateful, is a bright feature in a character by no means admirable.   The real name of the man was Malloch; and it may be taken as characteristic of his pseudo-refinement that he thought fit to change it, partly no doubt to get rid of the homely guttural, partly perhaps in foolish irritation at the coarse and clumsy wit which had transformed it into Moloch.   He had exercised himself in versifying even before he left Edinburgh; but it was not till 1724 that he produced his first notable piece,—as it happens, the only thing by him which is still remembered—the ballad of *William and Margaret*.   It was suggested, as Mallet himself declares, by the lines repeated by Merry-Thought in *The Knight of the Burning Pestle :*—

> "When it was grown to dark midnight,
>   And all were fast asleep,
>   In came Margaret's grimly ghost,
>   And stood at William's feet."

Mallet's ballad belongs to the same class as Hamilton of Bangour's *Braes of Yarrow*, to which however it is much inferior.   It may be described as an attempt to graft the elegance and classicism of the Queen Anne poets on the structure of the ancient ballad.   The way in which Mallet handles the old lines on which he worked is instructive :—

> "'Twas at the silent, solemn hour
>   When night and morning meet;
>   In glided Margaret's grimly ghost,
>   And stood at William's feet."

Every fresh touch here is in the eighteenth century spirit, and tends at least as much to weaken and to destroy the simplicity of the old ballad as it does to add to its smoothness. The moralising of the third stanza is also a departure from the ballad style. An artificial age had little to learn from Mallet even if he had continued to write in the strain which first won him a name. But he barely touched that string again. He is the author of another ballad, *Edwin and Emma,* and of a song to a Scotch tune, *The Birks of Endermay;* but the ballad is thoroughly artificial, and the song is one of those in which the substantive is always fitted with its orthodox epithet. The poet warbles about the smiling morn, the breathing spring, the tuneful birds, the feathered songsters, soft raptures, the verdant shade.

The example of Thomson carried Mallet away upon a new path. His *Excursion,* published in 1728, was suggested by Thomson's *Seasons,* then in progress and partly issued; indeed the imitation of subject and rhythm is shameless. There is however between the two a wide difference. *The Excursion* has all the faults of *The Seasons* more deeply accentuated. There is the same lack of unity, and there is besides a clumsiness in mediating transitions with which Thomson cannot be charged. On the other hand, we fail to find the fidelity and the insight which redeem *The Seasons.* Mallet could not trust himself to simple delineation of the ordinary scenes of nature: he attempted to make up by loudness of style and inflation of thought for that which he was half conscious of lacking in penetration. Fire must blaze, thunder rattle, death strike, to give interest to the page. In nearly all his longer pieces the storm is Mallet's unfailing resort in difficulty. The reason lies on the surface: of all natural scenes, a tempest is the one to which it is easiest to give the semblance of poetic dress.

But *The Excursion* was an early work, and it remained possible that maturer years and larger experience might enable Mallet to produce something better. He did so in *Amyntor and Theodora*, published in 1747. It was originally written for the stage, but was altered into the form of a narrative poem in blank verse. It contains a quantity of flowing and by no means unpleasing verse; but the sentiment is sickly to the last degree and the whole atmosphere of the poem unwholesome.

In the interval between these two works Mallet had engaged in a variety of literary ventures. In 1731 his tragedy of *Eurydice* was represented, but obtained little favour. The characters are ill drawn. Possessing few individual features they stand out, not as living beings, but rather as abstract types. Their utterances too are frequently turgid. Nevertheless *Eurydice* is not without merit. The story is interesting and clear, there is progress from scene to scene, and unexpected vigour in the language. Much the same may be said of the later tragedy of *Mustapha*, written with a political aim, and first acted in 1739. Mallet was one of the dependants of Prince Frederick, to please whom he held Walpole up to opprobrium in the character of Rustan, and represented the King in the person of Sultan Solyman as the dupe of that intriguing statesman. The piece, owing to its political complexion, was popular for a short time; but it had not enough of merit to preserve it permanently. The poisoning of the Sultan's mind is too childishly easy, and the *dramatis personae* are poor. Another tragedy, *Elvira*, acted at Drury Lane in 1763, was written also with a political end in view; but on this occasion it was in the interest, not of the opposition, but of the Bute government. The masques, *Alfred*, which he wrote in conjunction with Thomson, and *Britannia*, are of mediocre quality. Both contain some pleasing but commonplace lyrics.

Mallet also wrote a prose *Life of Bacon*, a trivial thing, worthless as an authority and hardly more important as a piece of composition.

He died in 1765. His works do little to adorn his country's literature, and his life did much to stain her name. Johnson says that " it was remarked of him that he was the only Scot whom Scotchmen did not commend."[1] He was a venal writer, a treacherous friend, a dishonest man. Whatever party could or would pay him he was ready to serve with his pen; and through his obsequiousness he made more by his writings than they were worth. He accepted from Bolingbroke the task of avenging upon Pope's memory his offence in publishing without authority *The Patriot King*. However Pope's guilt may be estimated, Mallet, his professed friend, was not the proper person to visit it upon him, especially as Pope was by that time dead. Mallet earned by this the bequest of the whole body of Bolingbroke's writings, published and unpublished. He was not even superior to the meanness of taking money for work which he never performed. He accepted, under the will of the Duchess of Marlborough, a legacy

---

[1] " He must have been *awful*," was the remark of one who heard this quotation.

of £1000 to write a life of the great Duke, spread reports of his progress in it, and died with nothing done. Such is the dishonourable life which Mallet's writings have done just enough to preserve from a merciful oblivion.

There still remain three of those who were named at the beginning as representatives of the Anglo-Scottish school. They differ considerably both from their fellows and from one another; but all agree in this, that they follow Thomson in the use of blank verse, and that they stand quite apart from the dominant school of Pope. One was the physician John Armstrong, a man both personally and in his literary work associated with Thomson. He was born in 1709 at Castleton in Roxburgh-shire, and, like Thomson, was an alumnus of Edinburgh University. Soon after he had finished his medical course he proceeded to London, where he intended to practise his profession. He was already known to a limited circle as a writer of verses; and, singularly enough, one of his first pieces, the subject of which is *Winter*, was, he says, just finished when Thomson's poem on the same subject appeared. Armstrong in this piece imitates Shakespeare rather than any contemporary; and though it is unimportant in itself, there is in its strength considerable promise. The sluggishness of his disposition and that splenetic cast of character which Thomson makes the leading feature of his portrait in *The Castle of Indolence*, combined perhaps with his addiction to literature, hindered his professional advancement. He attempted to further it by a treatise on a medical subject in 1737; but whatever good that might have done him

was more than balanced by a licentious poem published
the year before, *The Economy of Love,* a poem in such bad
taste that even the author, who was a man by no means
squeamish or ready to detect faults in himself, saw the
propriety of curtailing it in a later edition of its more
offensive parts. In the year 1744 he published *The Art
of Preserving Health,* a didactic poem in blank verse. It
is too little to say that this is Armstrong's most memorable work, for it dwarfs all else that he has written.

The Art of Preserving Health is divided into four
books, and consists in all of rather more than 2000 lines.
It sinks or rises according to the nature of the subject
immediately in hand. The first book, on air, admits of
comparatively free handling; the second, on diet, draws
from the poet a complaint expressed in a few fine
lines :—

> "A desart subject now
> Rougher and wilder, rises to my sight.
> A barren waste, where not a garland grows
> To bind the Muse's brow; not ev'n a proud
> Stupendous solitude frowns o'er the heath
> To rouse a noble horror in the soul."

The practical in this section prevails unduly over the
poetical. Medical maxims in verse are inevitably dry,
utterly misplaced, and, it may be suspected, less accurate
than if they had been given in prose. It was far from
being Armstrong's native instinct to indulge in sounding
language not particularly charged with meaning; but he
was sometimes forced to do so to atone by the semblance
of poetry for the absence of the true poetic spirit. He did
it occasionally when the temptation was less urgent; but
this evil trick, which he had partly caught from his con-

temporaries, was never a habit with him. One point in his medical advice in this second part deserves to be mentioned. He inculcates temperance in drinking, yet recommends an occasional debauch as necessary to enable a man to meet the claims of society. The manners of the time stand revealed in this more vividly than in all the moralist's denunciations of excess.

The third book is concerned with exercise, which the poet again complains of as intractable. The subject of the fourth is the passions. It is here that Armstrong has the freest scope, and here accordingly are found his finest passages. The power of the lines on melancholy must be felt by everyone. It is singular how clearly they betray, through a very different measure, the same hand that wrote the concluding stanzas of the first canto of *The Castle of Indolence.*[1] They are however superior :—

> " The dim-ey'd Fiend,
> Sour Melancholy, night and day provokes
> Her own eternal wound. The sun grows pale ;
> A mournful visionary light o'erspreads
> The chearful face of nature : earth becomes
> A dreary desart, and heaven frowns above.
> Then various shapes of curs'd illusion rise :
> Whate'er the wretched fears, creating Fear
> Forms out of nothing ; and with monsters teems
> Unknown in hell. The prostrate soul beneath
> A load of huge imagination heaves ;
> And all the horrors that the murderer feels
> With anxious flutterings wake the guiltless breast."

The man who wrote thus had a sympathetic insight into suffering ; and Armstrong's poem throughout gives evid-

---

[1] Those stanzas, which are descriptive of various diseases, were written by Armstrong for Thomson's poem.

ence of a marvellous power of realising the effects of disease as if he himself felt them. Perhaps however the finest lines he ever wrote are those descriptive of the plague in England. The passage is too long to quote as a whole, but the following extract from it will give some idea of its strength and elevation :—

> " It seem'd the general air,
> From pole to pole, from Atlas to the East,
> Was then at enmity with English blood.
> For, but the race of England, all were safe
> In foreign climes ; nor did the Fury taste
> The foreign blood which England then contain'd.
> Where should they fly ? The circumambient heaven
> Involv'd them still ; and every breeze was bane.
> Where find relief ? The salutary art
> Was mute, and, startled at the new disease,
> In fearful whispers hopeless omen gave.
> To heaven with suppliant rites they sent their pray'rs ;
> Heav'n heard them not. Of every hope depriv'd ;
> Fatigu'd with vain resources ; and subdued
> With woes resistless and enfeebling fear ;
> Passive they sunk beneath the weighty blow.
> Nothing but lamentable sounds was heard,
> Nor aught was seen but ghastly views of death.
> Infectious horror ran from face to face,
> And pale despair. 'Twas all the business then
> To tend the sick and in their turn to die.
> In heaps they fell : and oft one bed, they say,
> The sick'ning, dying, and the dead contain'd."

Armstrong continued to write poetry from time to time for many years after the publication of *The Art of Preserving Health*. His *Benevolence*, *Taste*, and *A Day*, the last an epistle addressed to John Wilkes, are the most considerable of his later poems. They are unfortunately in the heroic couplet, a measure over which Armstrong had much less mastery than he possessed over blank verse. The best of them is *Taste*, which is described as "an epistle to a young critic." It is marked by vigorous understanding and independence of judgment. From its subject and the nature of the opinions expressed, it is akin to Armstrong's prose volume, *Sketches or Essays on Various Subjects*, published under the pseudonym of Launcelot Temple in 1758. The best of these essays are critical, and the criticism is distinguished by its very modern cast of opinion. The essay *Of the Versification of English Tragedy* deserves the highest commendation. The writer says of Shakespeare that he had "the most musical ear of all the English poets," a judgment as honourable to his discernment as its expression at that time was to his courage. In 1770 he collected a number of his productions in two volumes of *Miscellanies*, which included a tragedy, *The Forced Marriage*, that had been rejected many years before. Some medical essays published in 1773 were Armstrong's last contribution to literature. He died in 1779, leaving, notwithstanding that he had never been successful either as poet or physician, a considerable sum of money scraped together by a thrift approaching penury.

Armstrong's early imitation of Shakespeare and his critical panegyrics on the great dramatist reveal his true leanings. He was indeed indebted to Thomson, but only in a slight degree; and the influence of his country is rather seen in the independence of the fashionable mode which it helped him to maintain, than in positive features of his style. He was one of the earliest students of the Elizabethans who went so far as to make them his models, and acknowledge them as supreme masters of poetic art. He owes to the school in which he studied the daring of his sombre imagination, the manliness of his style, and the strength of his verse.

Another of the band of Scots who cultivated blank verse was Robert Blair, author of the once famous and even now by no means forgotten poem, *The Grave*. Differing from Armstrong in most things, he agreed with him in this, that his leading characteristic was strength, and that he learnt the secret of this strength by a study of the Elizabethans. Blair was born in Edinburgh in 1699; and after an education at the university of his native city, followed by further study in Holland, he became a minister of the Church of Scotland, and in 1731 was appointed to the parish of Athelstaneford. As he was followed by John Home, author of *Douglas*, this parish had the somewhat unusual honour of cherishing two poets in succession.

Blair is said to have made his first attempts at verse in that *Edinburgh Miscellany* of 1720 which contained also the early efforts of Thomson and Mallet. Previous to his settlement at Athelstaneford, he had composed a poem to the memory of William Law, professor of philosophy in the University of Edinburgh, whose daughter he afterwards married. He had also already begun *The Grave*, but it was not published till 1743. The author had little time to prove what more he might be capable of doing. He died in 1746, leaving behind him a son, afterwards Lord President of the Court of Session, whose career proved that strength of understanding and stern morality were hereditary in the family.

The Grave immediately acquired a great popularity;

and though time has obscured its fame, it is still spoken of with respect by critics who cannot be suspected of undue sympathy either with Blair's country or with his tone of thought. Part of its vogue was doubtless due to considerations other than literary. A religious subject presents to an author the great advantage that, if he only avoids outspoken heresy, he will secure some audience irrespective of his merits; and if he shows real ability that audience generally remains faithful. Thus throughout the religious world, and especially in Scotland itself, where a gloomy Calvinism predisposed the people to a favourable reception of his dismal theme, there already existed a taste which could be gratified by such verse as Blair's. Further, there may be detected in universal human nature some traces of the ghoulish spirit. Horrors have for most men more or less of that morbid fascination which draws people to visit morgues, and glut their eyes on monstrosities of all kinds, and which Plato has noted in a familiar passage of the *Republic.* And about the time when Blair wrote, this unwholesome love of the gloomy, if not the ghastly, was unusually prevalent. It is visible not only in Blair's countryman Armstrong, but in Young, author of the *Night Thoughts.*[1]

The choice of such a subject as the grave does not necessarily imply anything morbid in the treatment; but it must be admitted that there is a morbid element in Blair's poem. He has no reticence about the worm

---

[1] It is probable that Blair was not indebted to Young; for although *The Grave* was not published till the year following the first of the *Night Thoughts,* Blair is known to have been in communication with publishers before any part of Young's work appeared.

that surfeits on the damask cheek of beauty, about the awful pangs attending the strong man's dissolution, or about the all-devouring appetite of the "great man-eater"; and he has been praised, most injudiciously, for being so out-spoken. Shakespeare has used much the same images; but a comparison of Blair with the parts of *Hamlet* and *Measure for Measure*, which he evidently had in his mind in more passages than one, shows at once what a change the stronger imagination has worked, how much more skilful is the execution, how much deeper the moral, how widely different in consequence the work of the two poets. Yet Blair has learnt not a little, and often has learnt well, from his master; and it is to his honour that he, a Scotch clergyman of a century and a half ago, is found imitating him at all. Often his lines sound simply like distant echoes of Shakespearian lines; but sometimes there is originality combined with a considerable share of Shakespeare's strength. And this is Blair's highest praise. At his best he shows a masculine vigour of language and an austere dignity of imagination more than sufficient to atone for the harshness of his verse, marred, nay, almost ruined, as it is by the abuse of the hypermetrical line. That there is virtue in the poem is proved by its richness in quotable and often-quoted lines—a feature which may be taken as one of the tests of good work. The best known is one which occurs in the description of the departure of good from the world at the sin of Adam, to return only in visits "like those of angels, short and far between." The simile is more familiar in the less happy form which Campbell gave it—"few and far

between."[1]   Blair's better manner is seen in the lines
which follow :—

> "Son of the morning, whither art thou gone?
> Where hast thou hid thy many-spangled head,
> And the majestic menace of thine eyes,
> Felt from afar."

But best of all that he wrote is the close of *The Grave*,
in which beauty of expression finely responds to beauty
of thought :—

> "'Tis but a night, a long and moonless night,
> We make the grave our bed, and then are gone.
> Thus at the shut of even the weary bird
> Leaves the wide air and, in some lonely brake,
> Cowers down and dozes till the dawn of day,
> Then claps his well-fledged wings and bears away."

The man who felt thus and wrote thus was, whatever
his limits, a true poet.   All the evidence points to the
conclusion that his limits were narrow.   There is no
trace of varied powers in Blair; but there is everywhere a guarantee that whatever else he might have
done with a longer life, he would have done nothing
weak.

Several of these men then show that they possess a
true poetic gift; and in the case of Thomson the gift is
a high one.   But there is a short, nameless, neglected
poem which contains verse of as high a quality as anything Armstrong or Thomson or Blair ever wrote.   The
poem in question, which is called *Albania*, was peculiarly
ill-fated.   Of the original edition only one copy is known

[1] There is, as Marsh points out in his *English Language*, a yet older
form of the simile in John Norris, who makes the angels' visits "short
and bright."

to survive, and that copy is provokingly sparing of information. It bears date 1737, and asserts that the poem
"was wrote by a Scots clergyman, who is since dead."
It does not reveal the name of this clergyman, nor that
of the editor. The dedication, apparently by the latter,
is addressed to General Wade. Leyden, from whom these
particulars are taken, included the poem in his little volume
of *Scottish Descriptive Poems;* and it is referred to appre-
ciatively by Scott in a letter to Joanna Baillie, and
quoted in a note to one of the ballads of the *Border
Minstrelsy.* But though it has long been known and
admired by a few, even Leyden's reprint did not bring
it into wide repute; so hard is it for a poem not associated with any known name to live.

Albania is very unequal. Within its short compass of
296 lines it contains one or two passages which would do
honour to most poets, while there are others little better
than prosaic. The promise of the better parts is all the
higher because it appears from internal evidence that
the author was only twenty-four years of age when he
wrote it; and a man who could write as this man wrote
at twenty-four might have been a king in letters had he
lived to the fulness of his powers. He combines however with the genius of a master many of the marks of
juvenility and inexperience. His success or failure de-
pends entirely on the subject immediately in hand: he
has not art to dress up the tamer passages. Where he
enumerates the elements of the wealth of Scotland he
grows prosaic; where his blood is warmed by the feeling
of patriotism or his imagination quickened by an inspiring
theme, he rises to excellence. His native power is shown

by the fact that the thought, though not always poetic, is always forcible; his art is sometimes crude, but his mind is never feeble.   The verse varies as the thought does.   At its best it is admirable; in the poorer passages it has neither variety nor harmony.   The lines best known are those quoted by Scott, descriptive of the spectre hunting in Ross :—

> "There oft is heard, at midnight, or at morn,
>   Beginning faint, but rising still more loud
>   And nearer, voice of hunters, and of hounds,
>   And horns hoarse-winded, blowing far and keen;
>   Forthwith the hubbub multiplies, the gale
>   Labours with rifer shrieks, and rifer din
>   Of hot pursuit, the broken cry of deer
>   Mangled by throttling dogs, the shouts of men,
>   And hoofs thick beating on the hollow hill.
>   Sudden the gazing heifer in the vale
>   Starts at the noise, and both the herdsman's ears
>   Tingle with inward dread.   Aghast he eyes
>   The mountain height, and all the ridges round,
>   Yet not one trace of living wight discerns;
>   Nor knows, o'erawed, and trembling as he stands,
>   To what, or whom, he owes his idle fear,
>   To ghost, to witch, to fairy, or to fiend,
>   But wonders, and no end of wondering finds."

This is powerfully imagined and powerfully expressed. It is however in passages of a patriotic cast that the writer usually shows at his best.   Of that description is the beautiful explanation of the late twilight in the North as due to the unwillingness of the sun to leave the land he loves.   He,

> "Looking back from the Atlantic brine,
>   Eyes thy glad slumbers with reflected beam,
>   And glitters o'er thy head the clear night long."

Such too are the opening verses, the finest in the poem. There is a music in some of the lines unequalled in the passages given above, and a fervour in the thought which, joined with the melody, gives the passage a place among the best blank verse of that age :—

> "O loved Albania! hardy nurse of men!
> Holding thy silver cross I worship thee,
> On this, thy old and solemn festival,
> Early, ere yet the wakeful cock hath crowed.
>   Hear! goddess, hear! that on the beryl flood,
> Enthroned of old, amid the waters' sound,
> Reign'st far and wide o'er many a sea-girt spot.
> Oh smile! whether on high Dunedin thou
> Guardest the steep and iron-bolted rock,
> Where trusted lie the monarchy's last gems,
> The sceptre, sword, and crown, that graced the brows,
> Since father Fergus, of an hundred kings:
> Or if, along the well-contested ground,
> The warlike Border-land, thou marchest proud;
> In Teviotdale, where many a shepherd dwells,
> By lovely-winding Tweed, or Cheviot brown:
> Nor ween I now in Durham's lofty spire
> To seek thee, though thy lov'd St. David's work;
> Nor where Newcastle opes her jetty mines
> Of coal; nor in strong Berwick; nor in Man,
> That never dreaded plague; nor in the wilds
> Of stony Westmoreland: all once thy own.
>   Hail, land of bow-men! seed of those who scorned
> To stoop the neck to wide imperial Rome.
> O dearest half of Albion sea-walled!
> Hail! state unconquered by the fire of war,
> Red war, that twenty ages round thee burned;
> To thee, for whom my purest raptures glow,
> Kneeling with filial homage, I devote
> My life, my strength, my first and latest song."

This assertion that *Albania* would be the author's last

song, as it was his first, seems unfortunately to have proved prophetic. Again at the end he repeats that it is patriotism alone which inspires his poetry :—

"Thus, Caledonia, many hilled ! to thee,
    End and beginning of my ardent song,
    I tune the Druid's lyre, to thee devote
    This lay, and love not music but for thee."

If he had lived long however, we may be sure that the fervour of soul which displays itself in such verse would again have enforced utterance. Much was lost in that early and nameless grave.

It may be desirable in a few sentences to recall the common features of this band of Scotchmen, and to mark what was new in their contribution to literature. All of them were distinguished by a certain independence of mind with reference to the literary fashion of the time : even Mallet needed but the example of Thomson to encourage him to cut himself free from it. The taste of the Queen Anne poets influenced them only to a slight degree. All of them too brought freshness with them, either, like Armstrong and Blair, as students of a manner which had fallen into disuse, or, like Thomson, from a new and original study of nature. It was precisely on these lines that the great literary revolution of the latter part of the century proceeded. The leaders of the romance movement turned for inspiration either to the Elizabethans or to the remains of our old popular poetry, as Blair and Armstrong, and as Hamilton and even Mallet had done The leaders of the natural school followed in the footsteps of Thomson, left the city and the study, and ceased to accept their impressions of nature at second hand. Like him, they trusted rather to

> "A heart
> That watches and receives."

Thus the men who have just been reviewed foreshadow, far more clearly than is commonly believed, the work of the revolutionary poets. They did not indeed do that work beforehand; but they helped greatly to make the doing of it possible.

CHAPTER IX.

THE LATER ANGLO-SCOTTISH SCHOOL OF THE EIGHTEENTH CENTURY.

JUST about the time when Thomson and his contemporaries were beginning to write, another set of poets of very different character were in their infancy. John Wilson, William Wilkie, Thomas Blacklock, and John Home were all born about the opening of the third decade of the century. William Falconer, William Julius Mickle, and James Beattie were some ten years younger. Later still came James Macpherson, Michael Bruce, and John Logan. These men differ widely among themselves, but still more widely from their immediate predecessors. It is curious that, except for dramatic composition, blank verse, the favourite measure of the former period, almost disappears in this. So too does that freshness of matter which is the chief merit of the elder group. It would seem that the longer continuance of close intercourse with England had made the weight of southern influence more heavily felt, and had checked the growth of native ideas.

The chronological order ought to be observed so far as to separate the first group from the rest; for it will be found that, while the characteristic of that group is merely imitation of the school of Pope, the later writers appear first to be groping after something new, and then to grasp it. This something new is romanticism. In the first group John Home, as a dramatist, stands apart. Of the others, Blacklock and Wilkie agree in this, that they touch hands at once with the English Augustan poets and with the ancient classical writers whom these professed to admire, and from whom they took their name. Blacklock is much the smaller man of the two. He has in truth little claim to remembrance except such as can be founded upon a pathetic story and an amiable and virtuous character. He lost his eyesight from smallpox in infancy; and struggling under this disadvantage he managed to acquire a considerable degree of learning. His favourite pursuit was poetry; an unwise choice, for he had no grandeur of idea to atone for the want of precision which must mark the descriptions of one who has never seen that which he describes. Even in an age when mediocre verse was more charitably received than it is at the present day, he would, but for the interest inspired by his blindness, have failed to attract attention. In virtue of that however, and of his personal charm, he was most favourably received. The kindly sceptic, David Hume, did all he could in his behalf, even surrendering to him his salary as Advocates' Librarian; and Spence, the professor of poetry at Oxford, to whom Blacklock was intro- duced by Hume, wrote an account of his life, character, and writings which made him known to the English public. Blacklock in his turn, at a later day, had it in his power to stretch a helping hand to Robert Burns; and the fact that he was partly the means of turning Burns from his design of emigrating, constitutes for him a stronger claim to remembrance than anything he ever wrote. For in truth neither his prose nor his poetry is of much value. In the poetry there is not one gleam of original power; and there is little even of that conventional prettiness which sometimes makes the minor poet mildly attractive.

Blacklock tried with song, ode, pastoral, and elegy to climb the gentler slopes of Parnassus; William Wilkie attempted to storm its steepest heights by means of his ambitious epic, *The Epigoniad*. He has fallen under a shadow of oblivion somewhat deeper than he deserved, though it is easily explained. A short poem moderately well done has a better chance to be read than a long one of the same quality, though the ability which has gone to the creation of the latter may be much greater than that devoted to the slighter work. *The Epigoniad* is moderately good; but it requires more than moderate merit to induce men to read [an epic in nine books.

Wilkie was a man with a history very similar to that of scores of his countrymen who, by dint of dauntless character and strong understanding, have conquered an unpropitious fortune. He was born in 1721, and was sent at the age of fourteen to the University of Edinburgh, but in the midst of his studies was recalled by his father's death to manage a farm and provide for a mother and three sisters. Most lads would have sunk under the burden, or at the utmost would have contented themselves with fighting successfully the battle for existence. But Wilkie never surrendered his ambitions. He carried through his studies to the end, was licensed, and received first the assistantship and afterwards the principal charge of the parish of Ratho. But he carried to the end of his life the marks of his stern struggle: it was the rude boorishness of his manner which induced Charles Towns-hend to say of him that "he had never met with a man who approached so near the two extremes of a god and a brute as Wilkie did."[1]

The Epigoniad, the great work of Wilkie's life, appeared in 1757. The nature of its reception might be guessed, even if there were no other evidence, from the tone of the *Dream in the Manner of Spenser*, which is really an apology for *The Epigoniad*, appended to the second edition of 1759. In this *Dream*, which consists of eighteen nerve-less Spenserian stanzas, the poet is brought before Homer, who asserts that Wilkie's merits are borrowed from him. Wilkie admits the charge, but replies with truth that others have borrowed full as much. There is some beauty in stanza xvii.:—

> " He smil'd, and from his wreath, which well could spare
> Such boon, the wreath with which his locks were clad,
> Pluck'd a few leaves to hide my temples bare;
> The present I receiv'd with heart full glad.
> Henceforth, quoth I, I never will be sad;
> For now I shall obtain my share of fame:
> Nor will licentious wit nor envy bad,
> With bitter taunts my verses dare to blame:
> This garland shall protect them, and exalt my name."

This poetical prophecy has not been fulfilled; time has only sunk *The Epigoniad* in a deeper obscurity. The choice of subject was unfortunate. The story of the siege of Thebes was one which could only have been made interesting to modern readers by a man of the highest

---

[1] *Alex. Carlyle's Autobiography*, p. 394.

powers.   It was doubtless Pope's Homer which inspired Wilkie with the ambition to write a classical epic ; but a translation of Homer, and a translation by Pope, was a very different thing from an original poem on a subject of ancient legend by William Wilkie.   There are numerous faults in Wilkie's composition—glaring Scotticisms, bad rhymes, incapacity to attain that neatness and point without which the heroic couplet is indefensible.   Worse than all is the absence of any great original ideas.   A short poem may have a sufficient *raison d'être* without much originality or largeness of conception, but an epic hardly. The minor faults of language and versification seem to have sprung chiefly from that irregular education which, although it did not prevent Wilkie from amassing learning, left him conspicuously unpolished.   The false rhymes are often, perhaps more often than not, explainable by the common Scottish pronunciation.   This has sometimes even led Wilkie to give a false form to his words ; for instance—

> " While here, in doubtful poise the battle *hings ;*
>   Faint is the host and wounded half the kings."

On the other hand, the narrative is clear and vigorous, the movement rapid, the style terse, and the similes not infrequently felicitous.   The following lines happily describe the dim hearing of a man wounded and apparently dead :—

> " The shouts tumultuous and the din of war,
>   His ear receiv'd like murmurs heard afar ;
>   Or as some peasant hears, securely laid
>   Beneath a vaulted cliff or woodland shade,
>   When o'er his head unnumber'd insects sing
>   In airy rounds, the children of the spring."

Wilkie's reputation for classical learning and his fame as a poet secured him, with the amusing inconsequence of the time, the post of Professor of Natural Philosophy at St. Andrews. Thither he went in 1759, and while there he published in 1768 his *Moral Fables in Verse*. They did not raise his reputation. He died in 1772, leaving behind him a name renowned for poetry and learning, but still more for eccentricity.

Yet another who founded upon the classicism of the Queen Anne poets was John Wilson, author of a descriptive poem entitled *Clyde*. He was born in 1720. His education, like Wilkie's, was cut short by his father's death, which occurred when he was fourteen years of age. Afterwards, young as he was, he supported himself by private teaching till, in 1736, he was appointed schoolmaster of his native parish of Lesmahagow. He seems to have been always given to literary pursuits; but it was not till 1764 that he published the only poem by which his name is still known. This poem, *Clyde*, was based upon an earlier and less elaborate piece entitled *Nethan*. Along with it was printed what the author seems to have considered, at the time at least, a more important work—a tragedy, now utterly forgotten, entitled *Earl Douglas*. Wilson's poetical career proved to be near its close when it seemed just opening. In 1767 he was made master of the grammar school of Greenock under the peculiar condition, according to Leyden,[1] that he would abstain from "the profane and unprofitable art of poem making." As Wilson was 47 years of age when this happened, and as the poems already published were

[1] *Scottish Descriptive Poems.*

therefore mature works, it is not probable that the world lost much by this enforced silence; but the action of the magistrates and minister who laid down this condition deserves to be commemorated wherever the name of John Wilson is mentioned. The poor muzzled poet lived till 1789; but for the rest of his life his name is blotted out of the annals of literature.

Clyde belongs to that class of poems of which the best known English examples are Denham's *Cooper's Hill* and Pope's *Windsor Forest.* It is descriptive of nature, not in general like Thomson's *Seasons*, still less as incidental to some action, according to the manner of epic poets, but of nature as seen in a particular locality. Poems of this class never have been and never will be popular. There is nothing, either in *Clyde* or in any of the pieces classed along with it, that can fairly be called artistic unity. It is true, as Leyden pointed out, that *Clyde* has the advantage over many descriptive poems of a definite starting point; but it labours under a disadvantage which at least balances this: it has no centre, there is no point round which the scenes are grouped, nor is there any continuous thread of feeling uniting them. The poet traces the Clyde from its source to the sea and along the shores of the Firth. Historical allusions, sometimes not unskilful, diversify the topography. But the topics are too numerous, and the effect of the whole is that of a series of sketches rather than of a finished picture. Among minor but still serious faults may be mentioned a want of mastery over the measure, the heroic couplet. It sometimes halts; and at other times, though it may scan tolerably, it betrays, in its ill-arranged pauses and needless Alexandrines, deficiency in the more subtle skill necessary to secure harmony. The diction is disfigured by Scotticisms, and the scantiness of Wilson's vocabulary shows itself in the frequent repetition of the same word within the space of a few lines. It is on the whole impossible to assign *Clyde* a high rank even in an uninteresting and generally feeble class of poems.

The last name of the first group is associated with one of those lofty reputations which occasionally spring up and decay like mushrooms. It is interesting because of its connexion with a species of literature which since the days of David Lindsay had been under a cloud in Scotland. John Home, the still famous and once flattered author of *Douglas*, was born at Leith in 1722. It has been already mentioned that he succeeded Blair at Athelstaneford. Soon after he had gone there he had a tragedy, *Agis*, ready for the stage, and made a journey to London to offer it to Garrick, by whom however it was declined. Again, in 1755, he set off on a similar errand with *Douglas*. Dr. Alexander Carlyle of Inveresk in his admirable *Autobiography* has given a vivid and irresistibly amusing account of the lofty expectations of Home's friends; of the difficulties and chances of the journey; how there was no satisfactory means of carrying the precious MS.; how the want was supplied; and of the final disappointment and indignation. Home and his friends however were not disposed to accept a second time the verdict of Garrick. London was the best place for such a masterpiece; but if London would reject the prophets Edinburgh might teach her a lesson. Towards the close of 1756 *Douglas* was acted there with great success, but not without results by no means agreeable to some of those concerned. It was bad that a minister of the Church of Scotland should write a play, worse that he should have the effrontery to put it upon an Edinburgh stage, worst of all that a number of his clerical brethren should be found to countenance him in his evil courses. The issue was a very serious ecclesiastical ferment. Those ministers who had witnessed the representation of Home's play were hotly attacked, and, according to their character, bent to the storm or defied it. Whyte of Liberton pleaded that he attended only once, and endeavoured to conceal himself in a corner to avoid giving offence. This contemptible plea was accepted in mitigation, and he escaped with suspension for six weeks. "Jupiter Carlyle," as, according to Scott, he was called, from having had his magnificently handsome person more than once painted for the king of gods and men, pursued a more manly course ; and though his courage involved him in much trouble and not a little professional danger, the cause of freedom was ultimately successful and the charge against him dismissed.

Home himself was driven, not altogether unwillingly, since the success of *Douglas* gave him the hope of making a living by his pen, to abandon his profession. He did so in June, 1757. He moved to London, where, shortly before his resignation, the once rejected *Douglas* had been acted with great applause. The playwright who had formerly been obliged to solicit the favour of managers was now courted by them. He had power of a more substantial kind too as a favourite of Lord

Bute, to whom he was appointed private secretary. After the success of *Douglas*, *Agis* was in 1758 put upon the stage; and two years later it was followed by *The Siege of Aquileia*. In 1762 Home retired once more to Scotland. His life there was marked by few events beyond the successive production of *The Fatal Discovery* in 1769, *Alonzo* in 1773, and *Alfred* in 1778. In that year his mental powers were permanently impaired through injuries caused by a fall from his horse. He survived till 1808, but produced nothing more except his prose *History of the Rebellion of 1745.*

So much of the flavour of Home's work has evaporated that the reader of the present day almost inevitably asks what is the secret of the extraordinary popularity he enjoyed in his own time. As far as Scotland is concerned, the explanation might be supposed to lie, and no doubt did in part lie, in the feeling of patriotism. Home was the representative Scot of literature, and the honour of his country was bound up with his. But he was scarcely less warmly received in England; and a Scot living in England under the Bute administration was not the person to arouse a prejudice in favour of himself. The explanation of the popularity must therefore be sought within Home's writings, not in external circumstances. It was probably due to the fact that his dramas appeal to sentiment; and thus, in an age when the appeal to reason had been somewhat overdone, they caught the fancy of the multitude. So long as the love of melodrama survives, and it is perennial, work such as Home's is sure of a temporary popularity.

The story of *Douglas* is briefly this: Lady Randolph

had in youth married privately a younger son of Douglas, between whose house and her father's there was a hereditary feud. Soon after the marriage her husband, her brother, and the priest who officiated were killed in battle. She gave birth in secret to a child. The nurse by agreement carried it away; but she was overtaken by a storm on the journey, and nothing more was heard of her or of the child. Thus all the witnesses had disappeared. The lady afterwards, to please her father, married Lord Randolph; but she is painted as the victim of a consuming sorrow. When the play opens the land is in commotion with a Danish invasion. A young shepherd, Norval, hastening to the war, saves Lord Randolph from assassins and is taken into high favour. He is followed by his supposed father, old Norval, through whom it is discovered that he is no other than Lady Randolph's son. This discovery is made in the absence of Randolph, and is concealed from him because the young Douglas is the real owner of the lands in Randolph's possession. Meanwhile Glenalvon, heir to Randolph and villain of the piece, observing the meetings between Lady Randolph and her son, fills the mind of Lord Randolph with jealousy. The latter watches, gets, as he believes, ocular proof of the truth of his suspicions, confronts Douglas after he has just left his mother's presence, fights him, and is on the point of being disarmed when Glenalvon treacherously wounds Douglas. The latter slays Glenalvon, but his own wound is mortal. Lady Randolph flees from the presence of the body and throws herself headlong from a cliff.

It is evident from this analysis that there is nothing

profound in the structure of the play. A secret marriage, a woman with her heart in the tomb, the return of a long-lost son, a villain to rouse a husband's jealousy—all are as ordinary as it is possible to conceive. Nearly every movement is conventional, and the characters are featureless. Lady Randolph's sorrow is weak and whining. It is intended that the reader or the spectator should admire her; but common sense suggests the possibility, unsuspected by Home, that it may be neither the best nor the most truly tender women who give up their lives to unavailing sorrow, and neglect the duty which lies before them. Norval has all the external features of the gallant and high-born youth. Even as a shepherd he displays the martial spirit. He is brave, generous, and high-souled. But there is nothing to distinguish him from other young men possessing these qualities. His almost miraculous readiness in arms, supposed to be a hereditary trait, is a conventional touch. Glenalvon again, who might have been the Iago of the play, is simply a vulgar scoundrel. All the dramatic capital of *Douglas* is exhausted in telling a sentimental tale; for characters there are none. There is, it is true, some poetry in the piece; but it is poetry of a weak type, pretty, but not beautiful, mildly interesting, but not rousing with new and great thoughts. The following lines are a favourable specimen :—

> "This is the place, the centre of the grove ;
> Here stands the oak, the monarch of the wood.
> How sweet and solemn is this midnight scene !
> The silver moon, unclouded, holds her way
> Through skies where I could count each little star.
> The fanning west wind scarcely stirs the leaves ;

"The river rushing o'er its pebbled bed,
Imposes silence with a stilly sound.
In such a place as this, at such an hour,
If ancestry can be in aught believed,
Descending spirits have conversed with man,
And told the secret of the world unknown."

There is nothing in Home's other plays to alter much the impression derived from *Douglas*. None of them vied with it in popularity, and most of them are clearly inferior. *Alfred*, the last, was also the weakest and least admired. It displays Home's sentimentalism in its least respectable light. His Alfred is a mere commonplace lover, risking for his passion not only his life but his kingdom; and by all the rules of probability he ought to have lost both. No wonder that an English audience rejected such a picture of their hero-king. It is in *Alfred* that we trace most clearly the influence of Shakespeare upon Home. The pretended frenzy of Ethelwida is modelled on the madness of Ophelia. It is to Home's honour that he revered Shakespeare and tried to form himself upon his example, at a time when able contemporaries viewed his admiration with little more than tolerance. Even David Hume in his correspondence shows that he would have been better pleased had his namesake adopted the French dramatists as his prototypes.

Agis, Home's earliest effort, is the least skilful in adaptation for the stage. The movement is languid, the interest weak, and the elements out of which the story is woven incongruous. The love-story of Lysander and Euanthe is an ill-disguised tag upon the tale of Spartan factions. The rhymed choruses are mere doggerel. *The Fatal Discovery*, the scene of which is laid away back in

Pictish times, is chiefly noticeable for the choice of subject, which indicates the influence of Macpherson.
Alonzo, which is said to have been best received of all
after *Douglas*, merely presents again the same characteristics in an exaggerated form. Here Home revels in
melodrama. There is much in it well calculated to win
a cheap and passing popularity; but it is nearly all tinsel,
which time has sorely tarnished. *The Siege of Aquileia* is
perhaps the best of all Home's works. It has the same
general character as *Douglas*, and in fact all its author's
plays; but the heroism is higher, the sentiment less
stagey. There is considerable vigour in the conduct of
the action, and the nobler passions are painted with
generous sympathy.

Home was a man who could harp with success upon
one string; but he could do nothing more. However
foreign it might be to his plot, he must either enlist the
spirit of sentiment or fail. To the true heroic he could
not rise. He had glimmerings of it in his soul, his heart
warmed to it, but he could not express it. Now that
the glitter of novelty is gone, it is easy to see that a
niggard nature had denied him the wreath of the *vates
sacer*. Johnson, whose scornful disbelief in Home is well
known, though he expressed his opinion in exaggerated
language, was essentially right.

But a literary reputation is rarely achieved without
some more or less real foundation; and Home's power
was real within the limits of sentiment. He was
master of a kind of pathos cognate to, yet different from,
that of *East Lynne*. He could at least make a martial
figure stalk with a gallant bearing across the stage, and

he could fill his mouth with sounding phrases. It ought in justice to be added that he has occasional lines of a high order. The comparison to the tide of all sorts of things that fluctuate is hackneyed enough; but it is very happily expressed in *The Siege of Aquileia :—*

> " For ebbing resolution ne'er returns,
>   But still falls farther from its former shore."

And in *Alonzo* there are one or two passages worthy of a better setting. The lines which follow might be not unfitly applied to the Homeric Achilles :—

> " Scorning his foes, offended with his friends,
>   Shrouded in anger and in deep disdain,
>   Like some prime planet in eclipse he moves,
>   Gazed at and feared."

And in another style this also is good :—

> " When sore affliction comes
> In the decline of life, 'tis like a storm,
> Which, in the rear of autumn, shakes the tree
> That frost had touched before ; and strips it bare
> Of all its leaves."

The younger men, Falconer, Mickle, Beattie, Macpherson, Logan, and Bruce, form a body in most respects heterogeneous, but presenting at least one feature in common. In all of them may be detected a more or less marked flavour of romance. The chief, perhaps in one or two instances the only interest attaching to their names will be found to rest in their blind groping after something more spiritually nourishing than couplets in the manner of Pope and on Pope's well-worn themes. The unanimity with which they sought the new field of romance is all the more remarkable because, in the group which preceded them and which was divided from them by only a few years, John Home was the only man who can be said to have shown any trace of a similar tendency. His sentimentalism was an element by no means alien to the time that was to come; but those who were strictly his contemporaries exhibited no such feature. They were on the contrary the faithful, almost the slavish followers of their immediate English predecessors. The later group however differed in an important respect from that of which Thomson was the centre. The earlier poets, as has been seen, carried with them into England the impress of their native country; in their successors that impress was much less conspicuous. The change of which they exhibited symptoms had begun to be general, and was no longer, except in the vernacular verse of Fergusson, a specially Scottish movement.

It will be convenient to take William Falconer first, for the double reason that he was the oldest man, and that his work, in external form at least, connects him more closely than any of the others with the Queen Anne poets. This man, the son of a barber, was born at Edinburgh in 1732. When a boy he was against his own will sent to sea. He had risen to the rank of second mate when his ship, which was trading between Alexandria and Venice, was wrecked near Cape Colonna. Falconer and two others alone escaped. His experiences on this occasion formed the subject of his one good poem, *The Shipwreck*. This piece, published in 1762, was one of the authorities from which Byron culled materials for his powerful description of the wreck in *Don Juan*.

Falconer's work is most unequal. The verse at its best has an admirably easy flow, and at the same time a nervous energy beyond the reach of the mere copyist. But there are two very different accents in it. One is that of imitated classicism. The parts descriptive of the scenes through which the ship passes are poor. To make them good would have demanded a culture which Falconer had no opportunity to acquire. The classical similes, introduced by way of illustration, and the hackneyed loves are also poor. The other accent is that of nature; and to this the poem owes the whole of its value. The fact that Falconer relates what he himself saw and endured gives reality to his descriptions and speed and fire to his narrative. Sometimes, nay often, he so overloads his verse with technicalities that it sinks to mere prose; but in the happier passages he succeeds in throwing over the hard facts of the sailor's life and lot the light of imagination. His fidelity to fact is the source of much that is bad, but likewise of all that is good in his poem. This too it is that connects him with the coming school. It is quite evident that he was troubled with no sense of discontent with the old. Versification and diction were imitated, as far as the author could imitate, from Pope; and where the matter suited he was ready to adopt the worst enormities of Pope's followers. But his choice of a subject introduced a vital difference. He had seen everything he described, had felt the agonies he painted, and was himself the hero of his poem.

The inequality of *The Shipwreck* is not confined to the ordinary rise and fall from passage to passage, but affects the main divisions of the poem as well. They are of widely different degrees of merit. The first canto is the poorest, because it is in great part occupied with matters not specially of a seafaring character, and does not therefore call forth Falconer's professional knowledge; the second, which, after a short introduction, is entirely occupied with the struggle against the storm, contains by far the greatest proportion of good work; the third and last, where a number of classical scenes pass in review, again sinks in quality. Falconer does not excel in happy isolated lines and expressions; yet he has a few, such as, for example, the picture in four words of the "long dark melancholy vale" between two monster billows. His scenes are of necessity prevailingly gloomy and terrible in their character. The following passage describing the conference of the officers in their extremity will give some idea of the nature of Falconer's style in such scenes:—

> "No blazon'd trophies o'er their concave spread,
> Nor storied pillars raised aloft their head:
> But here the Queen of Shade around them threw
> Her dragon wing, disastrous to the view!
> Dire was the scene with whirlwind, hail, and shower;
> Black melancholy ruled the fearful hour:
> Beneath, tremendous roll'd the flashing tide,
> Where fate on every billow seem'd to ride—
> Enclos'd with ills, by perils unsubdued,
> Great in distress the master-seaman stood!
> Skill'd to command; deliberate to advise;
> Expert in action; and in council wise."

Falconer could also paint well the contrasting picture of the peaceful departure of the vessel from port:—

> "Uptorn reluctant from its oozy cave,
> The ponderous anchor rises o'er the wave.

> High on the slippery masts the yards ascend,
> And far abroad the canvas wings extend.
> Along the glassy plain the vessel glides,
> While azure radiance trembles on her sides:
> The lunar rays in long reflection gleam,
> With silver deluging the fluid stream. "

Falconer wrote poetry both before and after *The Ship-wreck;* but of all his productions this is the only one of merit. His *Ode on the Duke of York's second Departure from England;* his *Demagogue,* a political satire on the elder Pitt, Wilkes, and Churchill; and the two or three minor pieces which go under his name, are all indifferent. An untimely death cut short his literary activity. He sailed in 1769 on board a ship which was never heard of after passing the Cape.

Falconer stands alone. The others may be best treated in two groups. Mickle, Logan, and Bruce all illustrate the lyrical revival; Macpherson and Beattie are more distinctly precursors of the romantic school.

William Julius Mickle, Falconer's junior by two years, had, like him, to bide the buffets of fortune; but not such buffets as could furnish him with poetical ideas or teach him that energy which Falconer learnt. He fled from importunate creditors to London; and there for some years led the miserable life of a man waiting the bounty of his Maecenas, Lord Lyttelton. The turning point of his fortune was reached when he was made corrector to the Clarendon Press. In the latter part of his life, notwithstanding his usual ill luck in commercial speculation, he was a moderately prosperous man. He died in 1788.

It is unnecessary, and it would be tedious, to notice

in detail all Mickle's contributions to literature. They are extremely varied. He meddled in the deistic controversy, attempted tragedy, translated an epic, wrote elegiacs, ballads, songs, and imitations of Spenser. Most of his work has more or less of the character of prettiness; none of it is powerful or original. His once celebrated translation of *The Lusiad* is now forgotten. Next to it perhaps the performance which had most fame in Mickle's own day was *Syr Martyn*, a weak imitation of Spenser, originally published under the title of *The Concubine*. It is full of archaisms which betray great ignorance of the history of the English language.

Mickle had not power to produce any long and sustained work, though he could, on the rare occasions when he deigned to be simple and natural, write a few graceful and pleasing verses. His odes of the Pindaric type have gone the way of nearly all such odes. Some of his songs have fared and have deserved to fare no better. If indeed we could credit him with that exquisite one, *There's nae luck about the house*, it must be admitted that he for once rose high; but if there is any force in internal evidence, scepticism on this point is justified. He has nothing else approaching it in merit, nothing at all resembling it in style. His most memorable production in the ballad class is *Cumnor Hall*, widely known through Scott's *Kenilworth*. It is here that he comes into contact with the new spirit. His ballad style is indeed far removed from that of the old minstrels, and it is often weakly rhetorical; but its smooth lyric flow illustrates the rise of a taste different from that of the classical school. Some of the elegies also show much grace of fancy and melody of verse. The influence of Gray is conspicuous in them.

Michael Bruce and John Logan were men considerably younger than Mickle. Bruce was born in 1746, Logan about two years later. They were friends in life; and their names have been associated since their death by a bitter controversy which has raged about the author-ship of the *Ode to the Cuckoo*. Absolute proof in favour of either cannot be looked for now. The facts are briefly these: Bruce died of consumption in 1767. Shortly after his death his MSS. were entrusted to Logan to edit; but it was not till 1770 that Logan issued a small volume containing seventeen pieces. These are described in the preface as a miscellany by different authors; but no guide to the authorship is given. In 1781 however the *Ode to the Cuckoo* was included in a volume of poems by Logan himself. It does not appear that his authorship was challenged during his life, though he survived till 1788. Many years afterwards local tradition was ransacked, and recollections of the *Ode* as the composition of Bruce were noted down. On this foundation violent attacks were made on the memory of Logan. That he was, to say the least, extremely imprudent and careless, and that a plausible case was made for Bruce, will probably not be denied by any one who has examined the question; but on the other hand, any one who reflects on the untrustworthy character of traditionary evidence many years old, will hesitate to brand Logan with the charge of so mean an act against his friend. It is true Logan's character was not in all respects above reproach. His conduct was so objectionable to the congregation of

South Leith, of which he was minister, that in 1786 he consented, in order to avoid litigation, to retire on an annuity. One of his offences however was the publication of a tragedy, *Runnamede;* and he was accused of nothing of a nature to make the charge of a peculiarly disgraceful literary theft more probable.

Whether it be Logan's or Bruce's, the *Ode* is entirely fresh, natural, and true. It delighted Wordsworth, and was not without influence on his own lyric addressed to the same bird. Neither of the writers for whom it is claimed did anything else equal to this. Among Bruce's acknowledged productions, there is much to praise in the *Elegy Written in Spring;* but his poem, *Sir James the Ross*, proves that he had not command of the ballad strain; and his poems in blank verse are value-less.

Logan, judged by his admitted compositions, was, on the whole, the better poet of the two; but as Bruce died so young this fact cannot be regarded as throwing light on the authorship of the *Ode*. Logan wrote prose as well as poetry. His sermons are smooth and pleasing in composition, but never very forcible or striking. The same merits mark his verse, and the same limitations. It is sweet, but cloying. His mind was elegant, not powerful. Effeminacy of taste is perceptible in his work generally, and especially in the melodramatic tragedy of *Runnamede*. But even if the *Ode* is not his, he deserves a niche in memory as the author of the fine song, *The Braes of Yarrow*, which, although it owes much to the older and more exquisite *Willie drowned in Yarrow*, has likewise high merits of its own:—

> "His mother from the window look'd
> With all the longing of a mother;
> His little sister weeping walk'd
> The greenwood path to meet her brother;

> "They sought him east, they sought him west,
> They sought him all the forest thorough;
> They only saw the cloud of night,
> They only heard the roar of Yarrow."

These men, as has been said, illustrate chiefly the lyrical movement. They could not but show also traces of the romantic revival so closely associated with it. Romanticism is however far more prominent in Beattie and Macpherson. Macpherson was the younger of the two, but he made himself felt in literature before Beattie. He was indeed, so far as Scotland is concerned, the true initiator of the romantic movement. This position must be assigned to him whatever view be taken either of the merits or of the authenticity of his chief works. Elsewhere too he had a greater influence over its development than is generally recognised.

James Macpherson was born in 1738. After an education at the Universities of Aberdeen and Edinburgh, when he was still only twenty, he published a bombastic poem entitled *The Highlander.* This and the other confessedly original works of Macpherson have been treated with scant respect both by his advocates and his assailants. Those who have accepted *Fingal* as a genuine translation from the Gaelic have generally argued from the poverty of Macpherson's acknowledged works his incapacity to produce *Fingal;* many of his detractors have contemptuously ranked both original works and professed translations in the category of the worthless. Two years later, in his *Fragments of Ancient Poetry collected in the Highlands of Scotland*, he made his appearance as a translator from the Gaelic. It was these fragments which first drew the attention of England in general, and more particularly of the Lowland Scotch, to the question of the remains of Gaelic literature in Scotland. A fund was raised by subscription, and Macpherson was sent into the Highlands to gather materials. The fruit of his search was the Ossianic poems as we now know them—*Fingal*, with some minor poems, published in 1762, *Temora* in the following year. They instantly attracted wide attention. They were translated into the principal languages of Europe; and they divided the learned into two hostile camps of believers and sceptics.

There are two questions about the Ossianic poems which ought to be kept carefully apart, though it has been too much the fashion to let the determination of the one colour judgment on the other. The first is the question of their genuineness; the second that of their merit.

The question whether these poems are translations may be regarded from two points of view. The Celtic scholar may inquire into their authenticity from the evidence of language, analysing and dissecting the " originals." The verdict pronounced upon such grounds must be the most authoritative. For any one however who is not a specialist in the Celtic languages it is only possible to state the result. This, in the present case, seems to be that the so-called Gaelic texts are documents made up to fit Macpherson's "translation." They are not wholly forgeries, but they have been much "doctored"; and there are innumerable indications in the language that even the genuine parts are far more modern than the date assigned by Macpherson.

This result agrees exactly with that reached by general criticism. It is no longer necessary to discuss the subject exhaustively; but the principal grounds upon which judgment proceeds may be briefly summarised here. There are two lines of argument. The first points out the inherent improbability of Macpherson's contentions, and the further doubt thrown upon it by the course which he chose to pursue; the second enforces this argument by a more detailed consideration of the poems as they appear in English.

As to the first: The date of *Ossian* carries us back to the third century; and we are asked to believe that thus early the Scottish Highlands produced one epic poem of six duans or cantos and another of eight. The production of such works implies no small degree of civilisation and refinement; and the proof that the Scottish Highlands had attained it is altogether wanting. And even if it could be believed that the poems had been written, their preservation through so many turbulent and distracted centuries would have been itself a marvel. The preservation of scattered and broken legends pointing back to a past as distant is a very different thing. Macpherson's position, therefore, being in itself so suggestive of scepticism, ought to have been supported by evidence of unusual strength. What he offered however was not more but less than ordinary evidence. The first requirement was that the MSS. should be made public upon which those extraordinary assertions rested.

It was treated as an affront. Macpherson's friends urged him to publish them; but, though he made preparations, so long as he lived they urged in vain. The verdict of scholars on the MSS. he left behind him has been already given.

When the contents of the poems in their English dress are considered, critical objections to the Macpherson story so accumulate that it seems wonderful that sane men should still be found, however prejudiced, to believe it, or any considerable portion of it. No one denies that there was and is in the Gaelic some foundation upon which Macpherson built; but from that admission to acceptance of his *Ossian* is a long step. In early poetry we expect simplicity and definiteness; in an early epic on the exploits of a great warrior we expect minute details of the fighting, descriptions of arms, the names of those he conquers, and particulars of the wounds by which they fell. There is little of all this in *Ossian ;* in *Fingal* singularly little; while the first part of *Temora*—and in a less degree the whole—reads as if it might have been Macpherson's answer to such objections. And while hardly anything is found that might be expected, a great deal appears which no one would have anticipated. The romantic love which holds such a conspicuous place in *Fingal ;* the chivalrous generosity to enemies and to the fallen, so inconsistent with the customs of early warfare; the frequent descriptions of nature not as an accessory, but for its own sake; the vagueness which pervades the whole, making it difficult to carry away a sense of the march of events—all these features point either to Macpherson's own invention, or to late composition in the Gaelic; and as the latter is a supposition for which there is no authority, it may be dismissed. It is safer to rely upon general considerations like these than upon special points like the mention of cars among a people to whom cars were unknown ; for that and similar difficulties might be explained on the theory of interpolation. The argument from omission too is inconclusive ; and yet most minds will be impressed by the point noted in Boswell's *Johnson,* that there is no mention of the wolf in *Fingal.* Of such arguments no single one may be in itself convincing, but united they press upon the mind with a weight not easily resisted.

Among the more general critical arguments no single point is more damnatory than Macpherson's treatment of the romantic passion of love. To find it in the poems at all would be surprising; to find it the main element in some, and a prominent feature in many others, rouses a suspicion of the strongest kind. It is only necessary to turn to the arguments which Macpherson prefixed to the poems to discover the astonishing part which this passion plays. Frequently the maiden, disguised, takes arms and fights for her lover. At some crisis the mail is torn from her shoulders, the white breast disclosed ; and the sequel is in the spirit of the orthodox modern novel. In *Fingal* we look for a breathless narrative of martial prowess ; but instead, we are introduced to heroes who are for ever thinking of some maid of snowy breast and softly rolling eye. As a rule, a fight is hardly begun when it is interrupted by some love incident.

But whether authentic or not, the Ossianic poems are facts. They exercised a powerful and very wide influence, and they ought therefore to be estimated with reference to their intrinsic merit. Of the many criticisms which have been given there are few which do not reveal prejudice on one side or the other; for as it was the tendency of the partisans of Macpherson to overpraise him, so we find that the minds of the sceptics were generally warped by their disbelief to undue depreciation. "Sir," said Johnson, "a man might write such stuff for ever if he would abandon his mind to it." If however *Fingal* had been purely "stuff," it would not have captivated a mind like Napoleon's. He was neither a poet nor a critic; but an intellect so piercing and energetic could hardly be taken with mere emptiness. Perhaps the kinship between the style of Macpherson and that of his own bulletins may partly explain the admiration; but still the admiration is worth noting. As regards the world in general, the explanation of Macpherson's wide popularity is doubtless to be found in the fact that he earlier than others gave it something for which it was waiting. England was destined at no distant date to be deluged with Mysteries of Udolpho, Frankensteins, Tales of Wonder, Scottish Chiefs, the multiform nutriment of the passion for the marvellous and the romantic. The countries of continental Europe felt the same need and grew a similar crop to satisfy it. Macpherson appealed to this passion. It has been seen that among his contemporaries and fellow-countrymen there were some who showed signs of the coming romantic movement; but he was the first in the English language who powerfully and decisively expressed it. And this must be set down as his signal merit. Far from being a mere translator, he was peculiarly original.[1] Not that Macpherson created

---

[1] Macpherson borrows, or, if the word is preferred, steals freely. It is the general spirit that is referred to as original.

the spirit of romance.   Three years after *Fingal*, Percy's
Reliques appeared ; and Chatterton's work and life were
both finished within eight years of the publication of the
Highland epic.   These three rank as contemporaneous
and independent pioneers.   To them principally we owe
the romantic revival.

It does not follow that Macpherson was a man of
great genius.   On the contrary, the range of his ideas
was so narrow that to read any one of his poems is to
become master of almost all that he had to say.   The
same expressions, the same images, and almost identical
situations recur again and again.   Repetition was affected
no doubt partly to give an aspect of antiquity; but in
Macpherson it goes deeper and discloses poverty of
mind.   Still, to deny him the praise of having well
expressed his few thoughts is unjust.   There is much
fustian in his style, and it speedily palls upon the ear ;
but the peculiar poetic prose which he formed for himself
has, in little bits, a powerful charm.   His descriptions of
scenery and of aspects of nature are often very beautiful.
We ask again and again why they are there, but he who
can forget their incongruity with a poem of the third
century must feel their truth.   Macpherson knew the
country in which he laid his scene, and caught something of the grandeur of its mountains and stormy seas.
His descriptions of female beauty are likewise good.
One of the best is that of Strina-dona :—

"If on the heath she moved, her breast was whiter than the down
of Cana ; if on the sea-beat shore, than the foam of the rolling ocean.
Her eyes were two stars of light.   Her face was heaven's bow in
showers.   Her dark hair flowed around it like the streaming clouds.
Thou wert the dweller of souls, white-handed Strina-dona."

His images have little variety, but they are often well applied, as in the following picture of a defeated army:—

" Now on the rising side of Cromla stood Erin's few sad sons ; like a grove through which the flame had rushed, hurried on by the winds of the stormy night ; distant, withered, dark they stand, with not a leaf to shake in the gale."

This pathetic tone is frequent ; much less common is that which we should expect to be prevalent, the tone of warlike exultation ; but we catch it in Ullin's war-song:—

" Son of the chief of generous steeds ! high-bounding king of spears ; strong arm in every perilous toil ; hard heart that never yields ; chief of the pointed arms of death : cut down the foe ; let no white sail bound round dark Inistore. Be thine arm like thunder, thine eyes like fire, thy heart of solid rock. Whirl round thy sword as a meteor at night ; lift thy shield like the flame of death. Son of the chief of generous steeds, cut down the foe ! Destroy !"

Such is the most remarkable and the most famous of literary forgeries. It is strange that two such notable forgeries as those of Macpherson and Chatterton should have come within a few years of one another, and still more strange that the forgers should both have been leaders of the romantic movement. Such coincidences are seldom the result purely of chance. In this instance the hidden impulse was given by the fact that the romantic revival had its roots in the far past ; and to men initiating it the idea naturally occurred of ascribing their works to the early times which they tried to reproduce. Harsh names have been given to both these men ; but there is less to blame in the act itself than in the means taken subsequently to support the imposition. This widely separates the case of Macpherson from that of poor Chatterton.

The "marvellous boy" was as much the superior of Macpherson in character as he was in genius.

About Macpherson's later career and works little need be said. The Ossianic poems procured him rewards much more substantial than mere fame. His subsequent writings were seldom either poetry or, like his *Ossian*, of the nature of poetry. In 1773 however he was so unwise as to publish a prose translation of the Iliad of Homer in the style of his *Ossian*. This translation, begun and ended in six weeks, was received as it deserved to be; and Johnson, on the occasion of the famous quarrel which drove him to provide himself with a cudgel, told the translator that his "abilities, since his Homer, were not so formidable." Macpherson died in 1796, and was buried in Westminster Abbey.

Somewhat later than Macpherson, but like him associated with the new romantic movement, was James Beattie, whose name is now remembered only through the poem of *The Minstrel*. He was born in 1735, and educated at Marischal College, Aberdeen, where, in 1760, he was appointed professor of moral philosophy and logic. His life was mainly a record of successive publications. Towards the close it was clouded by the premature death of his two sons, the elder of whom, a youth of much promise, left some literary remains in prose and verse, which were published with a touching memoir by his father in 1799. In the same year Beattie was struck with paralysis, and he died in 1803.

Beattie's odes are feeble echoes of *The Bard* of Gray and *The Passions* of Collins; his *Judgment of Paris* is mere rhetoric; his imitation of Shakespeare's *Blow*,

blow, thou winter wind is chiefly remarkable for the number of technical faults compressed within so narrow compass. *The Minstrel* itself is more noteworthy as a symptom than for its intrinsic merits. Beattie's purpose was to trace "the progress of a Poetical Genius, from the first dawning of fancy and reason, till that period at which he may be supposed capable of appearing in the world as a minstrel."[1] The nurture of this poetical genius is significant. His opening mind is fed upon tales of knight, swain, and maid, fairy, fiend, and monster from the old ballads. He drinks in at the same time the influence of rural nature, whose melancholy and terrible aspects are, in the true spirit of modern romance, as captivating as her smiles and sunshine. In more points than its Spenserian stanza *The Minstrel* resembles *Childe Harold*, also the picture of a poetic mind, but of a much more masculine one than Beattie's. Edwin, the "strange and wayward wight" of *The Minstrel*, has several of the milder features of the Childe; and the same air of affectation pervades and vitiates both poems. But none of the greater attributes of Byron's work can be ascribed to Beattie's. The strains of the latter are smooth and pleasing, but not strong. His thought is nowhere great; it verges on originality, but is never conspicuously fresh and new. *The Minstrel* besides is defective in the execution of its plan. The idea at the root of it was a happy one; and Wordsworth subsequently gave partial proof of what might be done with it. But Beattie did not really carry out his purpose. The figure of Edwin remains a mere

[1] Preface to *The Minstrel*.

shadow; and the reader cannot be said to behold the growth of a mind whose features are nowhere brought before his eye.

Besides this fundamental defect, which affects the whole, it is impossible to overlook the great inferiority of the second book to the first. This second book describes the opening of doubt of man and virtue in the innocent mind, and thus impinges upon topics which Beattie had already handled in his prose; for in the *Essay on Truth* (1770) he stood up as the champion of orthodox belief against the sceptic Hume. Neither in prose nor in poetry did he deal with the subject successfully. Probably therefore little has been lost from Beattie's failure to fulfil his design of adding a third book on the more mature experience of *The Minstrel;* it is very questionable if he had the necessary depth. He is most happy when in the first book he delineates the effect of natural scenery upon the poet's mind. He shows in an occasional line the influence of Shakespeare; but he is more indebted to Gray and to Percy's *Reliques.* The following description, though the verse is marred by the monotony of the pause, is good of its kind; and if the rest of the poem were equal to it, Beattie would deserve much higher praise than has been given to him :—

> "But who the melodies of morn can tell?
>   The wild brook babbling down the mountain side;
> The lowing herd; the sheepfold's simple bell;
>   The pipe of early shepherd dim descried
>   In the lone valley; echoing far and wide
> The clamorous horn along the cliffs above;
>   The hollow murmur of the ocean tide;

The hum of bees, the linnet's lay of love,
And the full choir that wakes the universal grove.

" The cottage curs at early pilgrim bark ;
    Crown'd with her pail the tripping milkmaid sings ;
The whistling ploughman stalks afield ; and, hark !
    Down the rough slope the ponderous waggon rings ;
    Through rustling corn the hare astonish'd springs ;
Slow tolls the village clock the drowsy hour ;
    The partridge bursts away on whirring wings ;
Deep mourns the turtle in sequester'd bower ;
And shrill lark carols clear from her aerial tower."

Such were the Scotchmen who, in the third quarter of the eighteenth century, contributed in English to the poetic literature of the country. They, the countrymen of Thomson, began by rejecting the example of Thomson, and reverting to somewhat servile imitations of a school already beginning to be discredited in England. This however proved to be but a passing phase; and if we take them as a whole, we see in these men a growing tendency to seek their models in earlier English literature, or even to go back for hints to the rude fragments of popular poetry. We see in them also evidence of a lyrical revival. And above all we see the beginning of the great romantic movement.

CHAPTER X.

ROBERT BURNS.

ROBERT BURNS was born near Ayr on the 25th of January, 1759. His father, William Burnes, was then and for seven years continued to be gardener to a gentleman in that neighbourhood. In 1766, that he might "have it in his power to keep his children under his own eye, till they could discern between good and evil,"[1] he leased from his employer the farm of Mount Oliphant. There he remained till 1777. It was during the years spent upon this farm that Robert Burns received the greater part of his irregular education. A beginning had been made even earlier. Robert was sent first of all to a school at Alloway Mill; but when, after a few months, the teacher received another appointment, William Burnes joined with four of his neighbours to engage a tutor for their children. The person selected, John Murdoch, was a man of sense and character; and though he left that part of the country about the year 1768, he had already exercised a considerable influence upon the future poet's mind. Robert was afterwards sent, at the age of thirteen or fourteen, for a summer quarter to Dalrymple. Either

[1] Burns's Letter to Dr. Moore.

for economy or because the services of both could not be spared, he and his brother Gilbert attended in alternate weeks.   In the following summer Robert went to Ayr to study English grammar under his former teacher Murdoch, who had now returned.   His time was so broken with calls to help with the harvest, that he was under tuition only three weeks.   During this time however he not only improved his English, but acquired a smattering of French, which he afterwards increased by his own industry.   This accomplishment, rare for a peasant's son, procured for Burns some notice; and there is evidence in his letters that he was himself not a little proud of it.   A short time which he spent in his nineteenth summer studying surveying at Kirkoswald completes the record of Burns's school education.   It seems meagre enough; but his real education was much better than it seems. We have to add the precept and example of a father who, when he could not procure professional instruction for his sons, "borrowed Salmon's *Geographical Grammar* for us, and endeavoured to make us acquainted with the history and situation of the different countries of the world; while, from a book society in Ayr, he procured for us the reading of Derham's *Physics and Astro-Theology*, and Ray's *Wisdom of God in the Creation*, to give us some idea of Astronomy and Natural History"; of a father who, moreover, "was at great pains, while we accompanied him in the labours of the farm, to lead the conversation to such subjects as might tend to increase our knowledge, or confirm us in habits of virtue."[1]   The truth is, Burns received a training not only superior to his

---

[1] Gilbert Burns.

position as a peasant's son, but better far than that of multitudes who stood much higher than he in social station. The attempt which has been frequently made by his countrymen to exalt him by exaggerating his difficulties in respect of training, is as unwise as it is uncalled for. It is a poor pedantry which regards education as a thing of schools and colleges only. Burns was fortunate in the moral and intellectual atmosphere of his early home. The material conditions of his life were doubtless painfully cramping—they left him, as we know, at times "half mad, half fed, half sarkit"—but it may be questioned whether the lack of a more extensive and systematic education ever seriously embarrassed his genius. It is possible, perhaps it is not even improbable, that he would have found more hindrance in a palace or a castle than in the "auld clay biggin'."

In the year 1777 William Burnes removed to the farm of Lochlea, in the parish of Tarbolton. There his family lived in comfort for four years; but afterwards there sprang up a dispute between the landlord and his tenant, which was decided by arbitration against Burnes. He died a ruined man in February, 1784. William Burnes was, it is clear, one of the noblest specimens of the Scottish peasant, a man in many respects closely resembling the father of Thomas Carlyle. It need not be matter for surprise that, notwithstanding a good head and a stainless conscience, fortune was uniformly against him. "I have met," says his great son, "with few who understood 'men, their manners, and their ways' equal to him; but stubborn ungainly integrity, and headlong ungovernable irascibility, are disqualifying circumstances; consequently, I was born a very poor man's son."[1]

Before the crisis in their father's affairs came, the brothers, Robert and Gilbert, had taken the farm of Mossgiel in Mauchline parish. This bargain also was a luckless one. Late seasons acting upon a cold soil seriously injured the crops of the four years which Burns spent upon the farm. A considerable part of the stock was lost, and the prospect was black. In the summer of 1786 Burns was on the point of sailing in despair for Jamaica. The means of paying for his passage he got by the publication, almost at the last moment, of a collection of his poems, which yielded him a profit of nearly £20. But for this he must, to use his own phrase, have indented himself. Well known as the passage is, what follows is best told in his own vivid words to Dr. Moore. "As soon as I was master of nine guineas, the price of wafting me to the torrid zone, I took a steerage passage in the first ship that was to sail from the Clyde; for 'hungry ruin had me in the wind.' I had been for some days skulking from covert to covert, under all the terrors of a jail; as some ill-advised people had uncoupled the merciless pack of the law at my heels. I had taken the last farewell of my few friends; my chest was on the road to Greenock; I had composed the last song I should ever measure in Caledonia, 'The gloomy night is gathering fast,' when a letter from Dr. Blacklock to a friend of mine overthrew all my schemes, by opening new prospects to my poetic ambition. The doctor belonged to a set of critics for whose applause I had not dared to hope. His

---

[1] Burns to Dr. Moore.

opinion, that I would meet with encouragement in Edinburgh for a second edition, fired me so much, that away I posted for that city, without a single acquaintance, or a single letter of introduction."

This was the turning point in Burns's life. It was also an event of the greatest importance for English literature. But here, unfortunately, other questions besides literary ones claim attention. "The terrors of a jail" menaced Burns because he was required to find security for the maintenance of his illegitimate twin children by Jean Armour. In recent times much mischievous nonsense has been written about the "allowance" necessary in estimating the frailties of men of genius ; and Burns has had more than his share of this allowance meted out to him. All that can wisely be said on this point was said long ago by Carlyle in one of the finest passages of moral criticism in the whole range of literature :—"Not the few inches of deflection from the mathematical orbit, which are so easily measured, but the *ratio* of these to the whole diameter, constitutes the real aberration. This orbit may be a planet, its diameter the breadth of the solar system ; or it may be a city hippodrome ; nay, the circle of a ginhorse, its diameter a score of feet or paces. But the inches of deflection only are measured; and it is assumed that the diameter of the ginhorse, and that of the planet, will yield the same ratio when compared with them! Here lies the root of many a blind, cruel condemnation of Burnses, Swifts, Rousseaus, which are never listened to with approval. Granted, the ship comes into harbour with shrouds and tackle damaged; the pilot is blameworthy; he has not been all-wise and all-powerful; but to know *how* blameworthy, tell us first whether his voyage has been round the Globe, or only to Ramsgate and the Isle of Dogs."[1] So much may fairly be said for Burns. His character may be, will be, found infinitely higher and nobler than that of the smooth, self-complacent respectability, unstained by any fault which human law or ordinary conventional opinion can lay finger upon, but unlighted also by any lofty aspiration or generous deed, and chargeable only before a higher bar with the one fault of a restrained and safe, but constant and immedicable selfishness. But all this should not blind us to facts, or lead us to juggle with truth. If we do, we shall fall into a mistake more serious than the mistake involved in that neglect of proportion which Carlyle condemns. The sins of a man of genius are not in themselves less than the same sins in smaller men : in that sense there need be and there ought to be no "allowance."

The facts in Burns's life which have roused all the controversy as to his character are really simple. Through his youth and early manhood he lived as might have been expected of his father's son, a life of simple virtue. While he worked at Lochlea he was allowed by his father the wages of other labourers, with which he provided himself with all his clothing as well as all his pleasures. At Mossgiel, which was a joint venture of the whole family, his allowance was £7 per annum, and his expenses never exceeded it.[2] Under such circumstances anything approaching debauchery was impossible. But already the germs of evil were in him. In 1781 he went to Irvine to learn the trade of a flax-dresser, and there mixed with

[1] *Essay on Burns.*   [2] Gilbert Burns.

company of a more libertine complexion than any he had yet met. His looser principles in later years, both as to drink and in his relations with women, may be traced back to this period. The first evidence of the evil influence exercised upon him was the birth of that illegitimate child celebrated in *The Poet's Welcome.* It was however a different affair which occasioned his trouble at the time when he meditated flight across the Atlantic. The mother of the twins whom he was called upon to support was Jean Armour, afterwards his wife. The affair was, and is, unfortunately too easily paralleled among Scottish rustics; but in Burns's case the fact that it was only one of several gives an ugly aspect of libertinism to his life.

Burns was always unfalteringly true in owning and facing his sin. From an honourable desire to spare her as much as possible of shame and reproach, he contracted an irregular marriage with Jean Armour. This was at the hour of his darkest fortune. He had neither the means of supporting his wife in Scotland, nor could he take her with him abroad. Consequently, Armour, the father, induced his daughter to destroy the papers establishing her marriage. Burns was wild with grief and indignation; and Wilson and other critics have taken his view of it and have denounced the conduct of Armour in unmeasured language. That he was subsequently harsh is indisputable; and that in persuading his daughter to take this course he showed callousness with regard to her reputation is also clear: but that his conduct was altogether without excuse is not so evident. It must be recollected that Burns's character was already stained; and that while public opinion among the lower classes in Scotland is shamefully tolerant of one such aberration, with respect to more than one it is tolerably severe. Armour had some ground for fearing that such a man might not be the best husband for his daughter. Again, with respect to the marriage, two points must be borne in mind. On the one hand it was valid: hence Burns's indignation with the father, whom he regarded as a man coming between him and his wife and thrusting them apart; hence too his charges of perjury against Jean. On the other hand it was irregular: hence the possibility of annulling it by the simple destruction of the document in Jean's possession—the sole evidence of its existence. The legal aspect of the act of destruction may be doubtful; but the inviolability of the marriage ought not to be pleaded by the apologists of Burns, seeing he was willing afterwards to earn "a certificate as a bachelor" by undergoing the discipline of the Kirk. The fact that any minister could have proposed to give him such a certificate shows how dubious at the best was the relation between Burns and Jean Armour.

It was under the pressure of this unhappy affair that Burns made his preparations for exile. How his prospects brightened and his plans changed has been already told. Nothing in all his history is better known than the story of his visit to Edinburgh in November, 1786. The critics, and that society which the critics did so much to rule, received him with enthusiasm. On the whole, the welcome they gave the poet was honourable alike to their judgment as critics and to their character as men;

yet it was not free from an element to which objection might be taken. Sometimes an unnecessary emphasis was laid on the *ploughman*, the inspired *ploughman*. With some exceptions, and these as was natural were just the best men, Edinburgh society betrayed a disposition, essentially vulgar and small-minded, to stare astonished, not at the man, but at the peasant. The marvel was less that the human mind should display such powers as those of Burns than that they should be lodged in a creature so low in the social scale. It must be added however that in later years this contemptible spirit has been far more conspicuous than it was at the poet's first appearance. Burns, on his part, seems to have borne himself in trying circumstances singularly well, steering an even course between the extremes of subservience and self-assertiveness.

That the critics recognised Burns readily and praised him generously was creditable to their penetration, but not surprising. The accepted models of excellence were indeed very different from anything he offered; but he was by no means unheralded. The whole poetic movement of the century in Scotland, from Ramsay with his editorial labours and original compositions, to Fergusson, seems now like a preparation for such a poet as Burns. The critical mind therefore was not unduly startled by his appearance. And again, the merit of his work was such, both in degree and in kind, that immediate recognition was easy and natural. The critics, on his first appearance in Edinburgh, judged him by the Kilmarnock volume, a small collection, but one containing quite an astonishing amount of his best work. *The Twa Dogs,*

The Holy Fair, the *Address to the Deil, The Vision, The Auld Farmer's New-Year-Morning Salutation to his Auld Mare Maggie, The Cotter's Saturday Night, To a Mouse, To a Mountain Daisy, The Bard's Epitaph,* and the Epistles *To James Smith* and *To a Young Friend,* though by no means all that is of high excellence in the Kilmarnock edition, were sufficient to stamp their author as a poet of extraordinary genius. Their merit also was simple and obvious. The very social position of the writer helped the critics to the right decision. They might have felt a shock of surprise if a man like John Home, cultured even as they were themselves, had written so; but it was natural that the man who had driven his plough over the daisy and ruined the mouse's nest, should sing of them.

The attention paid to Burns in the capital, and the more solid gains reaped from the Edinburgh edition, sufficed to change his whole life. He remained in Edinburgh during the whole of the winter of 1786-87. The company he associated with was mixed. He consorted now with the leaders of society, now with spirits humbler but at least as congenial. Among the latter his chief associate came to be William Nicoll, a master in the High School, whom Burns has graphically described as possessing a mind like his body—"he has a confounded strong in-kneed sort of soul." In truth, the man's faults were conspicuous, his merits were chiefly, though not altogether, the creation of the poet's fancy. Association with him did Burns an injury both in himself and in his relation to the higher society. Their regard for him was already on the wane when in May he left Edinburgh for a tour on the

Border.   The summer passed in renewed visits to Edinburgh and tours in the Highlands.   Some of his biographers and critics have been distressed to find that his
travels were productive of so little verse, and needlessly
puzzled to account for their barrenness.   The truth is
obvious that Burns was not one of those who deliberately
sit down to make a description.   Much as he loved
nature, he loved humanity more; and though no one
described better than he, his best descriptions are always
called forth by some theme to which they are merely incidental, and they derive half their beauty from their setting,
or from the sentiment imparted to them by the subject.
Purely descriptive poetry was in the main a growth later
than the days of Burns.

The following winter, 1787-88, Burns again passed principally in Edinburgh.   But though he enjoyed the society, im-
measurably more brilliant and varied than Scotland yielded
anywhere else, he had always the good sense to see that
the life was one which could not last.   The Edinburgh
volume yielded him a sum variously stated at from £400
to £700—a difference which may probably be accounted
for largely by the mode of computation, whether gross
or net profit be taken, whether the amount he possessed
on leaving Edinburgh or the amount paid by the publisher be understood.   At any rate he was in a position
of comparative ease and comfort.   To his brother Gilbert,
who was still struggling at Mauchline to support himself
and his mother, he lent about £200.   With the rest he
determined to stock a farm.   A Dumfriesshire gentleman,
Miller of Dalswinton, whose name is well known in connexion with the history of steam navigation, offered him

any of his unlet farms at a rent to be fixed by the poet himself. It is almost needless to say that the honourable liberality of the landlord was met by an equally honourable fairness on the part of the tenant. Burns made careful inquiries, fixed upon the farm of Ellisland, had it valued by two men of practical skill, and offered the rent which their judgment sanctioned. Mr. Miller accepted it, and Burns imagined himself settled for life. As a further step towards his settlement he made a public profession of marriage with Jean Armour. She was not immediately able to accompany him to Ellisland, where he resided from the middle of June, 1788; but she followed him there in December. For a few months after she joined him Burns was happier than at any other period of his life.

It was only however for a very short time that he trusted exclusively to farming for his livelihood. Before he left Edinburgh he had made interest to secure an appointment in the excise; and was soon, through the influence of Robert Graham of Fintry, one of the Commissioners of the Scottish Board of Excise, made " gauger " for the district in which he lived. The well-meant attempt to combine two occupations proved unfortunate. The farm was necessarily left largely in charge of servants, and, partly at least from that cause, was unremunerative. The melancholy which always beset Burns, and which was deepened by the sense of his ill success in the struggle for life, drove him to excesses which at the beginning of the Ellisland period he was careful to avoid. After four seasons he threw up the lease and removed, towards the close of 1791, to Dumfries.

Henceforward Burns was dependent upon the excise. His income from this source had not hitherto exceeded £50 a year: on his removal to Dumfries it was raised to £70. The prospect of further promotion was clouded by his imprudent expressions of sympathy with the French revolution. How far these expressions permanently injured him is not clear; but it is certain that their consequences were humiliation and mental anguish, and the obscuring of that "star of hope" whose light he so sorely needed. It must be admitted that the servant of state who so far forgot himself as to send a present of cannon to a power on the verge of war with his own country, put those who were set over him in a difficult position; and it would seem that the fault was rather that of society for thrusting such a being as Burns into the position of an excise officer, than of his superiors, who could scarcely pass over unnoticed so wild a freak. For this and other causes the closing years of his life were years of sad decline. His own conduct at this time has been severely condemned. Currie says much and suggests far more as to the personal degradation of Burns. It is pretty certain however that he judged too harshly. Burns was at no time a model of correct respectability; but he was never a habitual debauchee. At the beginning of the Dumfries period, as at the beginning of his residence at Ellisland, he was most careful of his conduct. It was the loss of hope that made him reckless in his life. The picture of his closing days is extremely painful. He who had once been the darling of Edinburgh society was to be seen on the shady side of the principal street of Dumfries, "while the opposite

side was gay with successive groups of gentlemen and
ladies, all drawn together for the festivities of the night
[a county ball], not one of whom seemed willing to
recognise him." [1]   He applied to himself the words, already quoted, of Lady Grizzel Baillie's song, " His bonnet
stood aye fu' round on his broo."   With him "life's day"
was now "near the gloamin'."   His mind was distracted
with anxiety as he contemplated the future of his family,
his body was worn with disease.   Under the double strain,
physical and mental, he sank, July 21st, 1796, at the age
of thirty-seven.

Adequate length of days is indispensable to the production of any monumental work.   Milton spent nearly
as much time as was granted for the whole mortal career
of Burns in what he regarded as a mere apprenticeship
to the art of poetry.   It is indispensable too that oppor·
tunity should be granted as well as time.   Those Greek
philosophers, whose superb wisdom, discredited for a
while by the youthful self-assurance of modern science,
is again enforcing recognition, insist upon nothing so
much as the need of σχολή to the noble mind.   In
this respect Burns was still more unfortunate than in the
matter of time.   His thirty-seven years of life were
shorter for effective purposes of art than the nine-and-
twenty of Shelley, hardly longer than the five-and-
twenty of Keats.

The crushing weight of circumstance becomes evident
when we contemplate his career from his first introduction to the world till his death.   A period of ten years
passed between the publication of the Kilmarnock edition

[1] Lockhart.

and the closing of the grave. For the purposes of poetry they ought to have been far more valuable than all the time that went before. They did not prove so. The cause must lie either in the man or his environment. The man was not blameless; but it was not he who was chiefly to blame. Few probably who study Burns will arrive at the conclusion that his was one of those minds which bloom early and fade early. A shrewd observer remarked of his great countryman and successor, Scott, that his sense was even more extraordinary than his genius. Strange as it may seem to many, the same assertion may be made with only a little less truth of Burns. He possessed a clear, penetrating, logical intellect, a sound and vigorous judgment. Once and again in his poems he delights the idealist with his flashes of inspiration; but just as frequently he captivates the man of common sense, who finds his own sober views of life expressed by the poet with infinitely more of force and point than he could give them. But sagacity of judgment and strength of reason are qualities which do not soon decay, which, on the contrary, seldom, in a rich mind, reach their full maturity till an age later than Burns ever saw. And the poems, when closely examined, give no countenance to the notion that Burns's mind was unprogressive. It is rather the limited quantity of the work and the fugitive character of the pieces that occasion disappointment. There is no sustained flight, there are rarely even pieces as long as he had written in his earlier days. On occasion, it is true, as in *Tam o' Shanter*, he proves that he can equal anything he had done before; but as a rule he contents himself with the

lyric cry, the expression of the moment's emotion in
song. It was unfortunately all that increasing responsi-
bilities and cankering disquiet left possible for him.
Even in his early manhood Burns had little enough of
peace of mind; but he had more than he ever afterwards
enjoyed. He had given fewer "hostages to fortune";
he had youthful buoyancy to lift him above his troubles;
and the result is seen in the fact that, notwithstanding
his youth, his work then is wider in its range than it
ever was in his more mature years.

The literary work of Burns is divisible into two
periods. The first ends with the publication of the
Kilmarnock volume; the second covers the rest of his
life. The division is justified by the marked difference
in the character of the work produced in the two
periods. In the earlier, satires, pictures of rural life, and
familiar epistles predominate; in the later, and in an
always increasing degree as time passed, songs take the
first place. In each period there is of course an inter-
mixture of the work characteristic of the other; but the
dominant note in either case is unmistakeable.

There has always been diversity of opinion as to the
relative merits of the two classes of poems, or what
comes to much the same thing, the two periods. Perhaps, on the whole, the loss of the songs would be the
more irreparable; but it may be questioned whether the
miscellaneous poems do not contain more conclusive
evidence of the greatness of the poet. The poems composed previous to the first visit to Edinburgh display
nearly all Burns's highest powers—his humour, his satire,
his pathos, the force and truth of his style, his insight

into nature. In so young a man nothing is more remarkable than their wide range. The scathing satire of
Holy Willie's Prayer, the humour tinged with pathos
of the *Address to the Deil*, the poetic feeling mingling
with the ludicrous in *Death and Dr. Hornbook*, the
elevation of *The Vision*, the beautiful descriptions of
simple rural peace and piety in *The Cotter's Saturday
Night*, the sympathy and exquisite purity of style in
the verses to the mouse and the daisy, the shrewdness
and sober-minded wisdom of the *Epistle to a Young
Friend*, the astonishing self-knowledge of *The Bard's
Epitaph*—these display a range and variety of power
which few poets have equalled.

Among the poems of Burns, the satires on the Kirk
form a class by themselves. They belong, by date of
composition, if not of publication, for the most part to the
earliest period of his authorship. Their force and bold-
ness at once drew, and have ever since fixed attention.
Their extraordinary merit as satires has been universally
acknowledged ; but, as is always the case where powerful
and important interests are touched, most diverse judgments have been passed upon their matter. Feeling was
naturally embittered when the questions immediately in
dispute were new; but the essence of the matter Burns
dealt with never grows old; and consequently we find
that to this day there are men who cannot read or think
of these satires with patience, or speak of them with
ordinary fairness. They are treated as writings, powerful
indeed, but disagreeable and of evil tendency, things which,
for the good of the world and for Burns's reputation as a
man, ought never to have been written, and should now

be sunk in oblivion. On the contrary, the world has been the better for them. To appreciate fairly the bearing of the satires upon the character of Burns, it is necessary to remember the circumstances in which they were produced. If they are judged in the abstract, the impression left is unfavourable to him as a man. There is much in them that would be better expunged; they frequently violate taste, jar upon the feelings, bring roughly forward matters which, as a rule, are better treated with a wise reticence. Some bitterness was inevitable at the time. When the satires were composed, in the words of Burns himself, "polemical divinity was putting the country half mad." The Kirk was split into the parties of the Auld Light and the New Light. The "Auld Lights" professed extreme Calvinism in doctrine, and supported a policy of unvarying conservatism with regard to the customs and observances of their religion; the "New Lights" professed more respect for works than for faith as it was apt to be understood, and advocated throughout a policy of liberalism. More than two hundred years had passed since the triumph of the principles of the Reformation under the leadership of Knox. Presbyterianism, forced throughout its first century into an unceasing conflict against an opposition often bigoted and unreasonable, and almost always injudiciously pressed, had emerged from the struggle victorious, but narrowed and intolerant. Another century of undisputed supremacy had done little or nothing to widen and humanise it. Grace and beauty are the growth of peace and prosperity. But peace had been so long denied to religion in Scotland that when it came the germ from which those qualities might have sprung was dead. They were altogether absent from the public religion of Burns's day. We must however distinguish between that and private religion, the simple unreasoned piety of the heart, the religion which ennobles the life of the individual and the family. This has rarely flourished in greater perfection than among the Scottish peasantry of a hundred years ago. Burns had seen it in his own father's home; and if he proved the relentless satirist of systematic Calvinism, he proved also the sympathetic poet and eulogist of fireside piety.

Official Presbyterianism, as Burns knew it, was of iron strength. It followed out its propositions to their conclusion with a merciless logic. More, perhaps, than any other system evolved by the wit of man, it insisted upon that *scientific* interpretation of the words of the Bible which Matthew Arnold deprecated; more than any other it neglected that deeper although less definite *literary* interpretation which he would have substituted. Consequently, it had become eminently non-human, in some aspects even inhuman. After two hundred chequered years, the Reformed Kirk itself stood in need of reform. It had done a great work for Scotland; but, even at the best, the good it brought had not been attained without a large price; and now the price exacted seemed to many, and to Burns among the rest, too great for the return. Theological fetters were cramping the movement and deforming the growth of the nation. The satires of Burns are to be regarded as blows struck for liberation from those fetters.

Burns then was a reformer as well as a poet. He was the Lindsay of his age, wielding with infinitely superior skill a weapon far keener than that which

Lindsay used with such effect against the abuses of Romanism. Like Lindsay, he is to be judged with reference to his main purpose and general effect. In satire rigid justice is impossible; there must be a brightening of the light on one side, a deepening of the shades on the other. What may fairly be demanded of the satirist is that he shall on the whole help that which is honourable and true. The question therefore is whether Burns did so or not. If his satires loosened the hold of religion in Scotland, it must be answered in the negative; if without striking at the principles of religion they helped to clear away abuses, to make religion more acceptable to the human heart, as well as the human head, more kindly and at the same time more truly rational, then, whatever the damage they may have done to the orthodoxy of the poet's day, the answer must be affirmative.

Burns was at heart a religious man. Carlyle, in most respects so appreciative and so keen-sighted, is surely in error when he says that Burns had no religion. "His religion, at best, is an anxious wish; like that of Rabelais, 'a great Perhaps.'" There is only a half truth in this. There are few things regarding the unseen of which Burns was sure. If he had been required to reduce his creed to definite propositions, for the truth of which he could confidently answer, they would not have been numerous. The outward acts of religion too attracted him little, and were but sparingly practised by him. He was not in the ordinary sense devotional. But his faith was constant in something higher than that which can be seen and handled, higher too than those prudential maxims of morality which are justified to the worldly mind by the plea that on the whole they tend to pleasure here. Burns was a creature of emotion. His patriotism, his friendship, and his love were all glorified by a magic light, the contribution of his own soul. But this light was to him the most real of all things; and the view of man and nature through such a light, the regulation of one's relations to them by it, is akin to religion. Burns nowhere attacks the fundamental principles of natural religion; on the contrary, there is much in his writings that supports them. In that beautiful though unequal piece, *The Cotter's Saturday Night*, which ought always to be remembered along with the satires, we see how deep and how sincere was the poet's sympathy with a pious life. In the satires themselves there is nothing to imply that this sympathy was affected or unreal, or that he ever lost it. There is no ridicule of the fundamental points of the Christian faith—unless we regard as fundamental the extreme deductions of Calvinism. What he satirises has been for the most part either changed or suffered to sink into oblivion. The greater part of the censure he has incurred has been on account of passages in which he merely expressed in the strongest and plainest language the creed of the ultra-orthodox; and it has been incurred because that creed will not bear expression. *Holy Willie's Prayer* is appalling reading; but the opening stanzas, the most terrible of all, are neither more nor less than a fearless and unshrinking statement of the doctrine of salvation as it was understood by the party satirised. If the satirist is blameworthy for stating the doctrine, still more are they blameworthy who preached it. This portentous theory long survived Burns's day. Men who are still in the prime of life can remember how the doctrine of election, with all its revolting accompaniments, used to be undisguisedly preached in country pulpits. Probably there are places where it is still preached; but for a long time the better minds of the country have been growing more and more hostile to such teaching, and utterances inconsistent with or openly contradictory of it have become increasingly frequent. The doctrine of eternal punishment has similarly lost favour. Burns had often heard it expounded in all its ghastly literalism—the

> "Vast, unbottom'd, boundless pit,
>   Fill'd fu' o' lowin' brunstane,
>   Whase ragin' flame, an' scorchin' heat
>   Wad melt the hardest whunstane,"

was preached as a physical reality. One of the herds in *The Holy Fair* describes it with such effect that

> "The half-asleep start up wi' fear,
>   An' think they hear it roarin'."

It was also the most important reality. The tidings proclaimed to an expectant people are "tidings o' *damnation.*" It is worthy of notice that Burns owed this telling point to the suggestion of that model of propriety, Dr. Blair. He had originally written "tidings o' salvation"; but the superior truth of the word suggested by Blair at once commended it to the poet.

Burns however satirised much more than mere doctrines. Observances, often as important as they, and the spirit underlying both creed and observance, which is always much more important than either, passed also beneath his censure. *The Holy Fair* is the most conspicuous example of his manner of dealing with objectionable observances. It is well known, and yet almost incredible, that he was painting from life. The practice of making the celebration of the Lord's Supper an occasion for gathering together the people of a wide neighbourhood had once been justified; and in days of great religious fervour the evils of such a gathering would be slight. The practice however, though habit had blinded people to the abuses incident to it, had long survived the existence of a degree of fervour capable of sanctifying it. The facts, those "stubborn chiels," were on the side of Burns, and his attack was the death-knell of holy fairs.[1] It is less easy to change the heart than the outward habits; and there is reason to fear that hypocrisy, self-righteousness, the belief in the efficacy of "faith" to cover the absence of "works," exist even now. Nevertheless, Burns has performed no greater service to his country than in his condemnation of these besetting sins, his holding up to the "unco guid" the mirror that reflects not appearance but reality, his contrast of the Hyperion faith and the satyr conduct.

It is seldom however that Burns's pieces are purely satirical. *Facit indignatio versum* can rarely be written of him. His great charm lies in the mixture of pure poetic feeling, or of careless fun and kindly humour, with the more biting satire. *Holy Willie's Prayer*, which per-

---

[1] Revivalism, I believe, occasionally resuscitates the Holy Fair even to this day.

haps for sheer force surpasses anything he ever wrote, unless it be the *Ode to the Memory of Mrs. Oswald o Auchincruive*, is almost the only example his works present of satire absolutely unmixed and unrelieved. In *The Twa Herds*, the humorous iteration of the metaphor of the shepherd and the flock, the references to "worrying tykes," "waifs and crocks," and "mangy sheep," the question whether the herds should be chosen for or by the brutes, move to laughter. The poet is more amused than angry as he writes. In *The Holy Fair*, the beautiful opening picture of the rising sun, the caller air, the hirpling hares, might stand in any other context; and the humours of the meeting fill the mind quite as much as the blast of the "Lord's ain trumpet." It is however in pieces unconnected with the Kirk that the satire passes most readily and freely into humour. Of such pieces the best is *Death and Dr. Hornbook*. There are few if any satires in the English language more poetical in character. From the point of view of the victim it is no doubt severe, even mercilessly severe; and personal satire of this description is so open to abuse, so dangerous in its consequences, that it is as a rule objectionable. Burns has been far more blamed for his Kirk satires than for this; but the moral right of the satirist to attack the Kirk seems far clearer than his right to set upon the luckless dominie and druggist Wilson.[1] Classes and class interests are generally powerful enough to defend themselves: if they suffer it is because they are faulty. But

[1] Of course *Holy Willie* comes under the same class with *Hornbook* as an attack upon an individual; though the general questions it raises are now far more interesting than the personal one.

an individual may be innocent and yet be powerless against the shafts of scorn and ridicule. Such was the case in the present instance. *Death and Dr. Hornbook* drove the victim, a pedantic but harmless person who eked out by quackery the scanty living he won as a village schoolmaster, from the place where he was settled. It is pleasant to know that the change improved his fortune; but the fact that he was for a time cast adrift upon the world, proves what a dangerous weapon personal satire is in a powerful hand.

If however we put aside the question of the poet's right to choose such a subject, it is evident that in *Death and Dr. Hornbook* the mood of Burns was more favourable to the production of poetry than in the more serious satires. The person satirised was too insignificant to rouse any deep feeling of anger. The whole treatment is light and playful. The key-note is struck in the opening scene—the poet "canty" with the "clachan yill," setting his staff to keep himself steady, and vainly attempting to count the horns of the moon. This introduction takes away the horror from the "something" that he encounters. Notwithstanding the awful insignia it bears, the apparition is a friendly one, and the conversation is easy and familiar. Throughout, the ludicrous prevails over the terrible. The satire is admirably mingled with humour. Hornbook and his pretensions are presented in so rich a setting of the writer's imagination that the mind dwells rather on the irresistible picture of the tipsy poet hob-nobbing with Death than on the doings of the village apothecary.

This mingling of satire with humour is characteristic

of Burns. Humour is the essence of some of his very best pieces and an element in most of them. It is this quality, combined with the vigorous narrative, which has given *Tam o' Shanter* such a firm hold on the popular mind; it is this which has led some of the most competent critics to rank *The Jolly Beggars* as the first of all Burns's works; it is this which gives their charm to the *Address to the Deil, The Twa Dogs, The Death of Mailie,* and most of the epistles. After the rare simplicity of style through which mainly he has been influential upon literature, there is no quality in Burns so conspicuous or so precious as this gift of humour. He had wit too as his works prove; but, like others of his countrymen, he was more distinguished for wit touched with that sympathy which makes it humour. The humour of the Scotch is generally described as dry; and a study of collections like that of Dean Ramsay at once explains and justifies the epithet. The humour of Burns however is warm rather than dry. The spring of it lies in the ready sympathy which enabled him to identify himself with the subject of his thought whatever it might be, human or brute, animate or inanimate. Sometimes this power of sympathy shows itself, as in the lines *To a Mountain Daisy,* in a tremulous sensitiveness which is not humorous. This piece has rather the accent of Wordsworth, who, with less humour than almost any poet of equal note, possessed a transcendent power of sympathy. It is also as heavily charged as Wordsworth's work with the "pathetic fallacy"; and the style is as pure and perfect as his at its best. If we turn to what is generally considered the companion piece, the verses *To a Mouse*, we detect the note of humour. The sensitiveness is equally delicate, the sympathy even more keen. The closer kinship to man in the mouse gives rise to the new feeling. The " wee, sleekit, cowerin', timorous beastie " is nearer to the heart of the poet than the " wee, modest, crimson-tipped flower."

Nowhere does the tenderness of Burns's nature show itself more clearly than in his treatment of animals. He was familiar with them, had made his dogs companions, had been fellow-labourer with the horse, was under the daily necessity of tending and caring for the cows and sheep. He had also known physical hardship, and could realise their sufferings from winter storm and cold. His references to animals are frequent, and almost always happy. Half the beauty of the fine opening stanzas of *A Winter Night* is due to the pitying sympathy with the animals exposed to the fury of the storm. The familiar Epistles are frequently enriched with graphic touches of a similar nature ; and the poems specially devoted to animals display in fuller measure the accuracy of observation and the exact knowledge revealed elsewhere by glimpses. *The Death of Mailie*, the lightest of them, borders on burlesque. There is more of tenderness in *The Auld Farmer's Salutation to his Mare Maggie;* and, though less popular, it is a far finer piece than the former. The youth and age of the animal are with exquisite feeling worked in with the youth and age of the man. They have shared both the pleasures and the toils of life; they have worn to crazy years together; the animal has been so intimately associated with the man's pleasures and troubles that he sees in her an animated chronicle of his life. But the best of this class of poems is undoubtedly *The Twa Dogs.* Here also man and the animal are made to reflect light upon one another; but in this instance the point of view is that of the dog, and the charm of the piece is not a little due to this inversion of the usual order. It is only at the opening that it can be said to be a picture of animal life; but that opening passage is perfect. Of all animals the dog has attracted most attention from men; but often as he and his ways have been described, they have never been painted with more ease and mastery, or with more truth, than in the beginning of Burns's tale. It was a happy thought to make the two interlocutors representatives of different social grades. Cæsar, the "gentleman and scholar," is in the canine world what Glencairn or Daer was in that above it. Luath, the ploughman's collie, stands to him in the relation of the poor but self-respecting peasant to these nobles. Up to the opening of their conversation every touch is, as all who know dogs must perceive, as true as it is vivid. Afterwards the piece is practically a criticism of two ranks of human society, which, however, frequently derives a special piquancy from the character of the speakers.

In the *Address to the Deil* Burns found a subject peculiarly suited to the play of his humour; and in few of his pieces does it show more favourably. As in the case of *Death and Dr. Hornbook*, he stands on a height of imaginative superiority and plays with his subject. The grotesque superstitions current in Scotland with respect to the personage celebrated by the piece become merely a vehicle for the finer thoughts of the poet. The concluding stanza, though hackneyed with quotation, possesses an indestructible beauty of sentiment—the hope for amendment in the prince of the powers of darkness himself, and the sorrow for even his fate. It has been less commonly noted that the second stanza, in which the poet calls upon Satan to listen to him, is in much the same spirit. He will not believe that even the devil is as black as he is painted, that even he can find pleasure in the torment of the helpless.

But for riotous luxuriance, *The Jolly Beggars* overtops all that Burns ever wrote. Probably no poem more graphic exists in literature. It describes what the writer had actually seen, and not otherwise would its extreme vividness seem to be attainable. Poosie Nansie's, where the revels took place, was a sort of tramps' lodging-house and inn at Mauchline. As Burns and two of his companions were one night passing up the street, themselves elevated, they were attracted by the sound of merry-making within, and at Burns's suggestion they entered. Thus he got his subject. It was a dangerous one. In meaner hands, in the hands of the mere realist, the result must have been a scene of sordid squalor. Nothing more strikingly shows the power of Burns than the fact that, without sacrificing truth, he contrives to give an altogether different aspect to it. The rags and dirt are there, but they are merely a foil to the mirth and jollity of the tattered revellers. They even heighten the general effect. Defiance of fate is nowhere more impressive, though also it is nowhere more common, than among those who stand on the very verge of destitution. Besides, the nakedness is due to the revelry : it is to quench their thirst that the beggars "toom their pocks and pawn their duds."

The Jolly Beggars is remarkable also for its truth of portraiture. No figure is elaborately drawn, but each has the attribute of life. The few lines of recitativo, which join the songs together, give the character in outline, and the song itself, which is always appropriate to the singer, fills up the sketch. The songs are ill fitted for the drawing-room, and some of the most vigorous passages are hardly suitable for quotation ; but the animal, man, not so much immoral as non-moral, was never better depicted. It is to be noticed however that even here, in a scene of the loudest and lowest revelry, Burns finds room and occasion for pure natural beauty. The meeting of the beggars takes place

> " When lyart leaves bestrew the yird,
> Or, wavering like the bauckie-bird,
>   Bedim cauld Boreas' blast ;
> When hailstanes drive wi' bitter skyte,
> And infant frosts begin to bite,
>   In hoary cranreuch drest."

No simile could be more happy than the comparison of the fate of autumn leaves in the northern blast to the bat's wavering flight. There is nothing forced in the introduction of the lines. The wintry landscape, so well drawn in a few words, forms a fitting contrast to the light and warmth in the haunt of the beggars. We have simply to forgive 'Boreas' : he and all his fraternity were the legacy of the earlier eighteenth century to Burns. Again, in the beautiful stanzas that open *A Winter Night* it is Boreas that "shivers thro' the leafless bower," and Phoebus that "gies a short-liv'd glower Far south the

lift"; and in many another fine passage there are similar
blots.   But they never seriously blemish the truth of the
pictures.

Burns's pieces are all so short that they cannot be
said to present conclusive evidence that he possessed
the power of poetic construction.   A song is but the
record of a single mood; there are no diverse elements
to be harmonised in it.   Even the longer poems—satires,
epistles, and tales—are almost all simple in structure.   In
The Jolly Beggars, more than anywhere else, he had to
grapple with difficulties of construction; and he did so
with conspicuous success.   Though the poem is not long
the number of figures is considerable; and they are presented not as units, but dramatically, as parts of a
whole.   The loves of the soldier, the tinker, the fiddler,
and the bard, with the quarrel which a common passion
stirs up between the "caird" and the "pigmy scraper,"
give colour and life to the entire poem.   And with
admirable judgment Burns closes it with a song which
sums up its philosophy, and is besides one of the most
spirited in our anthology :—

> "See the smoking bowl before us!
>   Mark our jovial ragged ring!
> Round and round take up the chorus,
>   And in raptures let us sing.
>
> *Chorus.*—"A fig for those by law protected!
>   Liberty's a glorious feast!
> Courts for cowards were erected,
>   Churches built to please the priest.
>
> "What is title?   What is treasure?
>   What is reputation's care?

If we lead a life of pleasure,
    'Tis no matter how or where!
            "A fig, etc.

" With the ready trick and fable,
    Round we wander all the day;
And at night, in barn or stable,
    Hug our doxies on the hay.
            "A fig, etc.

" Does the train-attended carriage
    Thro' the country lighter rove?
Does the sober bed of marriage
    Witness brighter scenes of love?
            "A fig, etc.

" Life is all a variorum,
    We regard not how it goes;
Let them cant about decorum
    Who have characters to lose.
            "A fig, etc.

" Here's to budgets, bags, and wallets!
    Here's to all the wandering train!
Here's our ragged brats and callets!
    One and all cry out, Amen!
            "A fig, etc."

Rapidity and skill of transition are noticeable in most of the work of Burns. Considering their modest length, his poems are surprisingly varied; for he was daring to the verge of temerity in binding together elements seemingly, but, as he proved, not really incongruous. One of his boldest ventures is the stanza descriptive of the soldier falling on the battlefield in the postscript to his *Earnest Cry and Prayer to the Scotch Representatives.* This is the heroic in the midst of burlesque. Yet though the rise to the lofty tone is abrupt and though it is maintained but for a moment, the stanza seems perfectly in place. But the best specimens of this power are to be found in the tale of *Tam o' Shanter.* It was with reference to this poem that Scott most justly remarked, "No poet, with the exception of Shakespeare, ever possessed the power of exciting the most varied and discordant emotions with such rapid transitions." The subject, the adventure of a drunken rustic with witches, promises merely amusement; but as the *Address to the Deil* is lifted above the vulgar superstitions on which it is founded, not merely by the masterly humour with which they are presented, but still more by refinement of sentiment exhibited, it might almost seem, in defiance of the theme, so the wealth of the poet's imagination clothes the tale of *Tam o' Shanter* in a magnificence not its own. It would be difficult to find a more beautiful series of similes than that contained in the well-known passage beginning, "But pleasures are like poppies spread." The storm is described with wonderful energy; and yet how rapidly the tone changes in it. At one moment the author's imagination is filled with the conflict of the elements. It is not the storm as felt by Tam, but the storm as conceived in the poet's soul that is depicted. The dreary night, the raging wind, the rattling showers, the thunder and the lightning—it is a storm that might have beat upon the head of Lear. "The speedy gleams the darkness swallow'd"—this is daringly imaginative, yet truer than photography. Scenes of winter tempest had a fascination for Burns. In *The Vision* he

notes a taste for them as one of his own characteristics :—

> "I saw thee seek the sounding shore,
>   Delighted with the dashing roar;
> Or when the North his fleecy store
>   Drove through the sky,
> I saw grim Nature's visage hoar
>   Struck thy young eye."

His pictures of such scenes are usually excellent. In
Tam o' Shanter however it would have been artistically
indefensible to let this spirit range unrestrained. After
the few terse lines descriptive of the storm we go back
to the hero, Tam, "skelping on thro' dub and mire," holding fast his bonnet, and "crooning" a song to himself.
In the apparition in Kirk Alloway we find the same
bold diversity. The dance of the witches and the piping
of their musician are ludicrous, the objects upon the in-
fernal altar are awful, even horrible, and carry us to the
very boundary of the permissible in art. But with exquisite
dexterity Burns secures the effect of further detail without
the shock it must have given. The concluding lines of
the passage,

> "Wi' mair o' horrible and awfu',
> Which ev'n to name wad be unlawfu',"

leave the imagination free to revel in those shadowy
terrors which, from their very vagueness, are so much
more fearful, though less ghastly, than the grim reality.

Poems of the class which have just been considered
were, as has been already said, for the most part the
product of Burns's youth. In after years he generally
contented himself with songs. He has himself told of his
youthful ambition, that he

"For puir auld Scotland's sake,
　Some usefu' plan or book could make,
　　Or sing a sang at least."

As years went on, fortune more and more restricted him to the literal singing of the song. He had cherished the dream of some time devoting his life to poetry. He could never realise this ambition; and it was fortunate for his own happiness, and fortunate for his country, that he had at his command a mode of poetic expression adapted better than any other to his condition. Burns was throughout his life intensely patriotic. Whatever seemed to him to redound to the glory of Scotland awakened his interest and fired his imagination. He had been led therefore, by his patriotic prejudice as well as by his native taste, to make a special study of Scottish poetry. He knew not only the work of men of established reputation, like Ramsay and Fergusson, but was intimately acquainted with the scraps of ballads and songs current among the peasantry. It became the task of his closing years to revise, amend, and complete those fragments, or to write entirely new sets of verses to old popular tunes. The inference that Burns attempted the writing of songs in his later days only would be a false one. On the contrary, the song, *Handsome Nell*, composed at the age of fifteen, was, he says, the first of all his performances; and ever afterwards he loved to touch the lyric string. But only in later days did he attempt song-writing extensively; and as he then wrote hardly any other kind of verse, the songs are naturally associated with the latter part of his life, just as the other poems are with the opening of his career.

In criticising the songs of Burns it is essential to take account of their historical connexions. They by no means stand alone. Both music and verse have their roots in the past: and they are not so much associated as fused together; for the songs of Burns, like Scottish songs in general, are emphatically meant to be sung. In collections such as those of Ramsay, Oswald, and Herd, we see the nature of the foundation upon which Burns built; but in his day, besides these song-books, there still lingered numberless fragments which had never been printed, and of which many are now lost beyond recovery. The copious remarks written by Burns on the margins of Johnson's *Scots Musical Museum*, and afterwards printed (with interpolations) by Cromek, prove the care with which he studied all the materials accessible to him. He was not the first in the field, but he was gifted with far greater genius than any who preceded him, and he had also more reverence for the forgotten poets whose remains he handled. He says in his first Commonplace-Book that it had given him many a heartache to reflect that the very names of the "glorious old bards" who had penned the ancient ballads were forgotten. Again, in a letter to Tytler of Woodhouselee, he says, "I invariably hold it sacrilege to add anything of my own to help out with the shattered wrecks of these venerable old compositions." Everyone knows, and probably few lament, that Burns's practice was widely different from his profession here; but there is ample proof that the reverence he professed was real.

From his habit of working upon the basis of the old popular songs it results that many of the lyrics which pass under the name of Burns are his only ·in part. The fact that he contributed extensively to the two great collections of Scottish songs, Johnson's *Scots Musical Museum* and Thomson's *Select Melodies of Scotland*, both undertaken in his time, had in this respect a great influence upon his work. Their object was to give as complete a body as possible of tunes and songs. Burns could not make the tunes, but he could and did fit them with words, or, where fragments of songs already existed, he could complete them. In many cases the precise relation of his work to the old cannot be determined; but enough is known to prove the enormous importance of his emendations and additions. He almost always improved what he touched; and he frequently purified what was loose and licentious.

Of all the songs added to, altered, or rewritten by Burns, the best known is *Auld Lang Syne*. In the letter to Thomson (Sept., 1793) in which he encloses it, Burns speaks of his version as "the old song of the olden times, which has never been in print, nor even in manuscript, until I took it down from an old man's singing." There is however no doubt that it is his own; and a comparison of his lines with the older versions in Ramsay and Watson illustrates his wonderful power of turning mediocre verse into beautiful poetry. *Somebody* is another exquisite song partly founded upon Ramsay but lifted far above the original. In *My Love's like a red, red rose*, Burns merely sought to give completeness to a fragment that might fairly vie with his own work. He supplied some lines to eke out the beautiful verses, *O gin my love were yon red rose;* but he needed no one to tell him that the old was in a higher strain than the new. The same inferiority to the original marks the alterations he made in the fine old song, *Aye waukin, O!* But this inferiority is quite exceptional. In most of the cases where we know the extent of the changes made by Burns, it is clear that nearly every touch is an improvement. In the still more numerous cases where the popularity of the version of Burns has driven the older song completely out of memory, we may safely infer the relative merits from the effect produced by the one upon the other.

One of the most difficult parts of Burns's task in thus piecing out the old remains of Scottish song was to bring his own thought into harmony with the original. He did it with admirable tact; and when he had any considerable groundwork given him there was no other course open. But just in proportion to the freedom given his hand, we find him ennobling the old tunes with verses of a strength, or a tenderness, or a humour, not to be found in the originals. Thus he found the old chorus,

> " My wife's a wanton wee thing,
>   My wife's a wanton wee thing,
>   My wife's a wanton wee thing,
>   She'll no be ruled by me."

Burns supplied the air with verses which do not need the apology with which he introduces them in his letter to Thomson (Nov. 8, 1792) :—

> " She is a winsome wee thing,
>   She is a handsome wee thing,
>   She is a bonnie wee thing,
>   This sweet wee wife o' mine.

"I never saw a fairer,
　I never lo'ed a dearer,
　And niest my heart I'll wear her,
　　For fear my jewel tine.

"She is a winsome wee thing,
　She is a handsome wee thing,
　She is a bonnie wee thing,
　　This sweet wee wife o' mine.

"The warld's wrack we share o't;
　The warstle and the care o't,
　Wi' her I'll blithely bear it,
　　And think my lot divine.

The "light horse gallop of the air," as Burns calls it in the letter to Thomson enclosing his own version, is not forgotten; but a world of grace and tenderness is added.   How magnificently again does he lift the materials of *Macpherson's Rant* out of the commonplace into the heroic in that "wild stormful song," *Macpherson's Farewell.* Compare

　　　　"I've lived a life of sturt and strife;
　　　　　I die by treacherie:
　　　　It burns my heart, I must depart,
　　　　　And not avenged be,"

with

　　　　"I've spent my time in rioting,
　　　　　Debauch'd my health and strength;
　　　　I've pillaged, plunder'd, murdered,
　　　　　But now, alas, at length,
　　　　I'm brought to punishment direct;
　　　　　Pale death draws near to me;
　　　　This end I never did project,
　　　　　To hang upon a tree."

The comparison is interesting, chiefly as illustrating the difference between the versifier and the inspired poet.

It was not the flat inanities of such lines as these that Burns had in his mind when he wrote the *Farewell*. The same character and the same event were before both writers—and the one produced this lukewarm trickle, the other that torrent of fire.

Thus it is always. Burns is happiest when the model he follows is such as to offer him not guidance, which means constraint, but suggestion. That he habitually sought for suggestion no one will ever regret who considers what he gained by doing so. To this habit is due the fact that of all songs those of Burns are the most singable. He was no musician, but he had enough of taste and knowledge to seize the spirit of the simple Scottish tunes. His correspondence with Thomson is full of penetrating remarks upon the connexion between the verse and the melody to which it was to be sung, and the constraint laid upon the writer of the words by the character of the music. In one letter (September, 1793) he gives a detailed and most interesting account of his manner of composition :—"'Laddie, lie near me,' must lie by me for some time. I do not know the air; and until I am complete master of a tune, in my own singing (such as it is), I can never compose for it. My way is : I consider the poetic sentiment correspondent to my idea of the musical expression ; then choose my theme ; begin one stanza; when that is composed, which is generally the most difficult part of the business, I walk out, sit down now and then, look out for objects in nature around me that are in unison and harmony with the cogitations of my fancy, and workings of my bosom ; humming every now and then the air with the verses have framed. When I feel my muse beginning to jade, I retire to the solitary fireside of my study, and there commit my effusions to paper; swinging at intervals on the hind legs of my elbow-chair, by way of calling forth my own critical strictures, as my pen goes on. Seriously, this, at home, is almost invariably my way." The whole correspondence with Thomson is worthy of close attention. It shows that the songs of Burns, though often rapidly written, were not mere sports of chance, but the conscious product of high art. It shows also that Burns could write vigorous prose as well as powerful verse, and deserves much of the praise sometimes uncritically lavished on the high-flown and unnatural letters to Clarinda.[1] Thomson's part in it however is trying to the temper. The self-sufficiency of his meddling emendations, which Burns too frequently accepted, is insufferable.

The crowning grace of the songs of Burns then, their peculiar fitness for their purpose, is seen to be the result of thought and conscientious care. It is in this respect

[1] Not only the letters to Clarinda, but the prose of Burns generally, has sometimes been extravagantly praised. To say that it is superior or even equal to his poetry is foolish exaggeration. It is however true that Burns wrote good, expressive, energetic prose. His letters, besides being extremely readable, are a mine of information as to his own character, and might therefore with advantage be more generally read. The letter to Dr. Moore is an admirable autobiographic sketch ; and in his general correspondence Burns, with less deliberate purpose, gives an equally clear revelation of himself. The most remarkable feature of his correspondence is the sympathy and adaptability it displays on the part of the writer. Probably without clear consciousness, certainly without hypocrisy, Burns takes a colour from the mind he is addressing; so that, if judged by the tone only, the several series of letters to different correspondents might be supposed to be the work of different men.

chiefly that they stand pre-eminent. There are English lyrics, notably some of the songs of Tennyson, which as poetry match the best of them; but there are no English lyrics, at least since the days of Shakespeare, that are so perfectly adapted to singing. But in his search for this quality Burns found more than he looked for. To the careful adaptation of the verses to the tunes we may ascribe, in part at least, their wonderful variety. He quotes in one of his letters (to Thomson, Jan., 1795) a critical dictum "that love and wine are the exclusive themes for song-writing." There needs only a reference to Burns himself to prove that this opinion cannot be maintained; but probably the proof would have been less conclusive but for his close study of the spirit of the tunes, leading to a delicate gradation of the sentiment of the verse. The truth is that the range of the song is just the range of simple human emotion; and Burns has covered nearly the whole of it. *Duncan Gray* is a song of pure humour. In the bacchanalian jollity of *Willie brew'd a peck o' maut* we have the only rival of *Toddlin' hame.* *Auld Lang Syne* is by universal acceptance *the* song of friendship. *Scots wha hae* is probably the finest patriotic song ever written. *Kenmure's on and awa'* and *Does haughty Gaul invasion threat* are different notes in the same key, the latter in a semi-playful tone which does not conceal its essential seriousness. In *Go fetch to me a pint o' wine* love is mingled with the heroism not of the patriot but of the soldier; while *Macpherson's Farewell* immortalises that of the outlaw. *Gloomy Night* is the expression of the heart of the exile. *A man's a man for a' that*, though its author declared it to be "not really poetry," is the special song of manly independence. The variety is almost endless. It remains indeed true that the majority of the songs are songs of love; but it would be a great mistake to suppose that there is no variety concealed under this general description. It is love of many kinds and sung in many keys, from the emotion not earthly at all of *Mary in Heaven*, to the sufficiently worldly note of *Hey for a lass wi' a tocher*, or the less sordid, but light and careless spirit of *Last May a braw wooer*, or the spirited defiance of *O for ane-and-twenty, Tam;* from the heart-broken youthful passion of *Ae fond kiss and then we sever*, to the calm but deep affection of the evening of life in *John Anderson, my jo*. The excellence is at least as conspicuous as the variety of these songs. The mere names of a few of the best are enough to impress the mind with their exquisite quality. Besides those already mentioned, the class of love-songs alone yields *Highland Mary, Behind yon hills where Lugar flows, My Nannie's awa, Mary Morison, Of a' the airts, The Posie, Flow gently, sweet Afton*, and *Oh, wert thou in the cauld blast*. These form a collection unrivalled in English literature. It must suffice to quote the last. Dr. John Brown, who possessed a critical faculty unsurpassed for delicacy, has declared it to be "the most perfect, the finest love-song in our or in any language; the love being affectionate more than passionate, love in possession not in pursuit." [1]

> "Oh, wert thou in the cauld blast,
>   On yonder lea, on yonder lea,
> My plaidie to the angry airt,
>   I'd shelter thee, I'd shelter thee:

[1] *Horae Subsecivae*, 2nd Series.

Or did misfortune's bitter storms
　　Around thee blaw, around thee blaw,
Thy bield should be my bosom,
　　To share it a', to share it a'.

　Or were I in the wildest waste,
　　Sae bleak and bare, sae bleak and bare,
The desert were a paradise,
　　If thou wert there, if thou wert there:
Or were I monarch of the globe
　　With thee to reign, with thee to reign,
The brightest jewel in my crown
　　Wad be my queen, wad be my queen."

Such are the works of a mind singularly rich in poetic gifts. They are all individually slight; even collectively they are by no means a full and sufficient expression of what was in the man. He entertained various designs of a more ambitious character; but he was never able to carry them out. Regret for the failure of his plans might however be wasted. It is in part at least to the fact that his poetry is, so to speak, so portable, that Burns owes his unequalled popularity. The circumstances of modern life are such that no long poem can penetrate the mass of the people. Picked men of the labouring classes may doubtless make themselves masters of Hamlet, or Paradise Lost, or Paracelsus; but the multitude never. We speak of some English poets as popular, and contrast them with others who are said to appeal only to a limited class; but no poet is popular in England as Burns is in Scotland, none appeals to the mass. There are degrees of narrowness in their audience, but it always *is* narrow. Burns on the contrary has been one of the most powerful educative influences of his country; and the fact may console us, as it would assuredly have consoled him, for any injury his reputation may, in the judgment of the academies, have sustained through the defects of his education or other untoward circumstances of his life.

There remain only one or two points that still call for notice. One is the curious charge of "provinciality" which has been brought against Burns by one of the most refined and penetrating of English critics, Matthew Arnold, and partly countenanced by another, Mr. Ruskin. Burns, says Arnold, lives in a world of Scotch drink, Scotch religion, and Scotch manners. For Burns, says Mr. Ruskin, the moon must rise over the Cumnock hills. This criticism has been conclusively answered by Mr. Nichol in his admirable essay on Burns. "Provincialism" means a narrowness of thought and sympathy, leading a man to take what is temporary and local for that which is eternal and universal. No man was ever entirely free from error of this kind; but it is strange indeed to charge specially with it the man whose sympathy embraced not merely the human race, but the mouse, the daisy, the very devil himself; and whose thought, remaining loyal to principles of order, was at war with all the mere conventions of his day, social, religious, and political. The secret of the error is to be sought in some confusion of mind as to the meaning of provincialism; and the words of Mr. Ruskin furnish the key. The charge that Burns must make the sun glint over the moors beneath his eye, the moon rise over the hills that bound his view—what is it but a charge that he uses the concrete instead of the abstract, the real and vivid in preference to the vague and un-known? Would he have been greater if he had made

the sun glitter on Soracte, or the moon rise over the
Alban Mount? Arnold's accusation rests on the same
fallacy. The atmosphere of Scotch drink, Scotch religion,
and Scotch manners, no more makes Dr. Hornbook and
Holy Willie, and Tam o' Shanter, and the glorious company of beggars provincial, than Falstaff's potations of
sack in an Eastcheap tavern make his humour local and
evanescent. The question in respect to Burns, as to
every poet, is, what is the quality of the jewel clasped in
the local setting? That the setting is local certainly
does not detract from its value.

As the use of a dialect naturally suggests provincialism,
it is not improbable that the language in which Burns
wrote had something to do with the charge thus brought
against him. Yet his employment of it is very far from
justifying the criticism. In regard to Burns's work
nothing needs more to be insisted upon than the
exquisite taste with which he varies the language,
because no important element of his poetic power has
been less appreciated. Mr. Ruskin, strangely enough in
view of the mistake into which he fell, pointed it out
years ago; but general recognition of it has been
hindered by the common acceptance of the judgment
that Burns's English verse is much inferior to his Scotch.
This judgment is in the main sound; but the inferiority
has been exaggerated, and the few conspicuous exceptions to its truth have been ignored. *To Mary in
Heaven* contains not one word of Scotch; nor does the
powerful and terrible *Ode Sacred to the Memory of Mrs.
Oswald of Auchincruive;* and in the song *Gloomy Night*
the one exception is the now half-Anglicised "bonnie." A

number of other excellent poems or parts of poems might be mentioned in which there is little or no Scotch. The truth is, Burns modified his language to suit his theme, and did it with inimitable tact and delicacy. He never forgot—or perhaps he never remembered, but native taste silently instructed him—that vernacular Scotch, though a dialect with a literature, was still a dialect. It was therefore in its nature colloquial. The development it had received was mainly such as fitted it to express the feelings, wants, and aspirations of unsophisticated people. Within its own limits it was admirable—strong, expressive, copious; but a literary language has to discharge many functions for which it was quite inadequate. Science, philosophy, all the apparatus of learning had to be sought outside its bounds. It was not even capable of expressing equally all the emotions of the heart. Though it contained words finely expressive of heroism and patriotism, these were sentiments not calling for daily utterance, and the vocabulary for them was consequently by comparison meagre. Naturally so; for the union had merged the national life of Scotland in that of England. Lowland Scotch was a speech which, while it traced back its lineage to the same root as southern English, had long developed on independent lines, but had now ceased to do so. It was no longer self-sufficing: the northern shoot had to be grafted on a southern stock.

It is obvious that this state of matters offered a golden opportunity to any poet capable of taking advantage of it. Barnes and Tennyson have shown that even the English dialects can be used with literary effect. But

an English dialect is a mere *patois ;* Lowland Scotch
with its generations of literary cultivation stands on a
different level. One of the great merits of Burns is
that he perceived more clearly by far than any of his
predecessors at once the extent and the limits of its
capabilities. It is highly improbable that he could have
enunciated the principle by which he guided himself;
but his works prove that he was, whether consciously or
not, guided by a principle. Ramsay and Fergusson were
not. They wrote English poems as well as Scotch;
but it is only now and then that we can detect a
reason for their choice of language. With Burns on the
contrary, as with Scott after him, it is only now and
then that we are baffled. He did indeed sometimes write
English when he had better not have written at all ; but
when he was really inspired he glided almost unobserved
—that is, by any one to whom the Scotch presents no
difficulty—from one to the other.

From the nature of the case we should expect that
the poems most deeply concerned with the daily life of
the peasantry—their hopes and fears, their interests and
amusements—would contain the largest proportion of
Scotch words ; and a very brief examination shows that
they do. Wherever the feeling is peculiarly homely,
wherever it appeals specially to men in their everyday
moods, there the vernacular element is richest and least
restrained. Poems devoted to rural observances, like
Hallowe'en, or poems of broad humour, like *Duncan Gray*, are
Scotch. The familiar epistles and the satires are likewise
rich in the vernacular. Humour, wherever it enters, has
a powerful effect upon the diction of Burns. Perhaps

this is best seen by contrasting the vocabulary of the lines *To a Mouse* with that of the lines *To a Mountain Daisy*. The lament for the ruin of the mouse's home has been already noticed as touched with humour; it is also deeply Scotch. The lines on the daisy, which are destitute of the humorous element, present far fewer difficulties to a person unfamiliar with the language.

In the same way, pity, tenderness, and playfulness are all expressed in Scotch. We see this in the sympathetic description of the cattle exposed to the storm in *A Winter's Night*, and in the more light and careless songs. We see it perhaps best by contrast in the deeper songs. Those whose keynote is tenderness, like *Of a' the airts* and *Oh, wert thou in the cauld blast*, are Scotch; but *To Mary in Heaven* is pure English. Here the idea of a dead love was felt by the poet to demand utterance in language more aloof from common life. And it is the same principle which prevails throughout. Wherever the sentiment is unusually elevated or unusually far removed from his habitual tone of mind, Burns's diction is English. It may be objected that the sentiment of Burns is never more elevated than in *Scots wha hae*, the language of which is Scotch. But it is not Scotch in the sense in which *The Holy Fair* or the *Address to the Deil* is Scotch. The words are all English—there is only an occasional dialectical variation in spelling and pronunciation. So too the song, *Go fetch to me a pint of wine*, which is as much a song of heroism as of love, shows Scotch near the vanishing point; and in *Macpherson's Farewell* there is little of Scotch but the chorus.

The best evidence however of the sensitiveness of

Burns to this principle of diction is to be found in pieces which are in part pronouncedly Scotch, but which vary with the changes of the subject. *Tam o' Shanter* is conspicuously such a piece. In it, as was to be expected, Scotch prevails. The introduction, the description of the potations of Tam, of the dance of the witches, and of the wild chase, are all rich in dialect. But the series of similes illustrating the fleeting character of pleasure are pure English; and so, except in pronunciation, is the picture of the storm at its wildest :—

> "Before him Doon pours all his floods;
> The doubling storm rolls through the woods;
> The lightnings flash from pole to pole;
> Near and more near the thunders roll."

In *The Vision* again the opening stanzas, and they are the finest, are pure Scotch; but the entrance of Coila chastens the poet's language. Though she is a Scottish muse he describes the glories of her mantle in verses essentially English, and her own words are English too. The same change of language is seen when we compare the first half of *The Cotter's Saturday Night* with the stanzas descriptive of the worship of the family and the patriotic prayer which closes the poem. The division is here marked with peculiar clearness. Even the Cotter's preparations for worship are narrated in Scotch; but from his utterance of "Let us worship God," the diction changes. Illustrations might be multiplied; but very frequently the change betrays itself in a line, perhaps even in a word. In such cases its character would not be obvious in quotation; but it reveals itself to

any one who is willing to read Burns with care and able
to read him with taste.

Of the many judgments which have been pronounced
upon Burns, three, of which two are in verse and one
in prose, have been specially distinguished for depth
and truth. The last is that of Carlyle. The other two
are respectively by Wordsworth and by Burns himself.
Wordsworth, in the beautiful stanzas *At the Grave of Burns,*
and in the *Thoughts suggested the day following,* contents
himself with setting his seal to the poet's judgment of
himself, which he declares to be all that is required
of the biographer. And still, after a hundred years, the
well-known lines of *The Bard's Epitaph* present the best
and justest view of the significance of his life :—

> "Is there a whim-inspirèd fool,
>   Owre fast for thought, owre hot for rule,
>   Owre blate to seek, owre proud to snool,
>   Let him draw near;
>   And owre this grassy heap sing dool,
>   And drap a tear.

> "Is there a bard of rustic song,
>   Who, noteless, steals the crowds among,
>   That weekly this area throng,
>   O, pass not by!
>   But with a frater-feeling strong,
>   Here, heave a sigh.

> "Is there a man, whose judgment clear
>   Can others teach the course to steer,
>   Yet runs, himself, life's mad career,
>   Wild as the wave?
>   Here pause—and, thro' the starting tear,
>   Survey this grave.

"The poor inhabitant below
  Was quick to learn, and wise to know,
  And keenly felt the friendly glow,
        And softer flame,
  But thoughtless follies laid him low,
        And stain'd his name.

"Reader, attend! Whether thy soul
  Soars fancy's flights beyond the pole,
  Or darkling grubs this earthly hole,
        In low pursuit ;
  Know, prudent, cautious self-control
        Is wisdom's root."

CHAPTER XI.

SIR WALTER SCOTT.

THERE is perhaps nothing more fortunate in the literary history of Scotland than the opportune appearance of the two greatest figures in its later annals. On the one hand, the country had long been ripening for them; on the other, the time was rapidly coming when the absorption of Scottish life in the wider life of England would make a distinctive treatment of northern subjects difficult, if not impracticable. Burns and Scott would have been impossible either much before or much after the time when they appeared. At an earlier period they would have found themselves cramped by the circumstances of the country; later, they would indeed have been free to work; but they would have found national characteristics in rapid process of obliteration.

The connexion between the history of a nation and its literature is nowhere more clearly shown than in the case of Scotland; for there it is not obscured, as it generally is, by the very continuity of the literature. We find in the life of the nation two great movements separated by centuries; and we find in its literature two great periods, also wide apart. We conjecture, and an examination of the facts justifies the conjecture, that there is here more than a coincidence. The older Scotland was the outcome of the War of Independence; and the older Scottish literature, from Barbour's *Bruce* to *The Complaynt of Scotland* and the lofty and sonorous Latin verse of Buchanan, owes its distinctive features to that great struggle. The later Scotland was created by the Reformation and the union with England; and the later Scottish literature, whether in the way of agreement or of opposition, shows deeply marked traces of the fact. But in both cases the literary response to the historic impulse was slow, just because in both cases the struggle was for very life. In the later instance it did not come fully till the close of the eighteenth and the beginning of the nineteenth centuries. Burns and Scott are the mature fruit of the teaching of Knox and of the accession of the Stuarts to the English throne. Burns has filled the popular imagination more than Scott; but it is Scott who is, in the most catholic sense, the representative of the mind of his country. It was he who, it has been well said, gave Scotland a citizenship in literature.

The facts of Scott's life need be recapitulated only in the briefest fashion. They are enshrined in a biography which has no superior in English, except Boswell's *Johnson*.

Walter Scott, who was the son of a respectable Edinburgh lawyer, was born on 15th August, 1771. A series of accidents threatened to cut him off in early childhood. His first nurse proved to be ill of consumption, which, but for the warning of a physician, she would probably have communicated to her nursling. Another nurse was on the

point of murdering him.   The malady which resulted in a
life-long lameness is hardly to be regretted, as it probably
spoiled an ordinary dragoon, and made a good poet and a
great novelist.   Scott in after years described himself
with truth as "a rattle-sculled half-lawyer, half-sportsman,
through whose head a regiment of horse has been exer-
cising since he was five years old."[1]   He was educated
in the manner usual at that time with Scotch boys of good
position, first at the High School, and afterwards at the
University of his native city; but owing to the uncertain
state of his health his attendance was irregular.   The
intervals occasioned by illness were spent in desultory
reading, and in picking up the ballads and legends with
which his frequent residence with friends on the Border
made him familiar; but, notwithstanding his own declara-
tion that he had since "had too frequently reason to
repent that few ever read so much, and to so little purpose," it can hardly be doubted that this unsystematic
self-education was more fruitful than any regular training
he could have received.   In the year 1786, when he was
apprenticed to his father, the non-professional part of
Scott's education, so far as it depended upon schools and
colleges, came to an end.   His service in his father's
office however was only preliminary to his adoption of
the higher walk of the profession of law.   He was called
to the bar in 1792.   It would be a great mistake to regard
Scott's studies in law as the perfunctory occupation of a
man whose best intellect was always given to other things.
He worked hard, and acquired not only, like his own
Jonathan Oldbuck, a mastery of the principles which

---

[1] Letter to Miss Seward, Lockhart, ii. 59.

happened to excite his interest, but also an extensive acquaintance with legal detail. It was owing not exclusively to the fact that he had other tastes, but partly also to accident, that he did not become a great lawyer. His application to professional studies, besides furnishing him with an exhaustless store of topics and illustrations, which he used in his writings generally with discretion, though at times perhaps to excess, gave his mind a discipline in habits of patience, order, and system, to which probably must be ascribed his extraordinary fertility.

At the time when Scott was called to the bar, and for years afterwards, he looked upon law as the profession by which he was to make his living and to rise in the world. He early developed literary tastes; but it was long before he thought of making literature, to use his own phrase, even his staff; and to the end of his life he never consented to let it become his crutch. Looking back however upon his early life it is easy to see that much which appeared at the time trivial or accidental was really a training of the best kind for what was to be his true life-work. The scenery, the ballads, and the legends of the Border, impressed upon him in his grandfather's house at Sandy-Knowe and his aunt's at Kelso, left deep and lasting marks on his mind. The journeys which he had to undertake into the Highlands in connexion with his father's business made him familiar with scenes and characters of another description. But it was in 1792, the year of his call to the bar, that he may be said to have also received, unknown to himself, his call to literature. It was then that, in company with Robert Shortreed, he made his first "raid" into

Liddesdale. The raid was repeated annually during seven successive years; and the fruit of these visits was that intimate knowledge of the geography of the Border glens, of the character of their inhabitants, and of the relics of Border literature, so abundantly manifested in his works, from the *Border Minstrelsy* to *Castle Dangerous*.

A purpose grew out of these originally purposeless or purely pleasurable excursions. Scott's mind was ready to burst into blaze with any spark, and did indeed catch fire at more than one point. He was at this time studying German. The wild ballads of Bürger caught his fancy; and in 1796 he made his first appearance in literature as a translator. Three years later followed the more important venture of the translation of Goethe's *Goetz von Berlichingen*. "Monk" Lewis was at this time at the height of his fame; and Scott, on the strength of his translations from Bürger, was asked to contribute to *Tales of Wonder*. Spenser, Ariosto, and Ossian, with a host of others of the romantic school, were likewise objects of his youthful study. All these elements of the literature of romance met in a mind already sufficiently sympathetic; and Scott's private history during these years deepened the impression they produced. His early and unsuccessful passion for Miss Stuart Belches, the memory of which clung to him till death, added that touch of the tragic which gives dignity to romance. But the eye accustomed to "the moonlight of romance" sometimes loses the more valuable faculty of seeing objects in the light of common day. Scott would probably in any case have been saved from this misfortune by his strong sense and vigorous character; but he soon had the additional safeguard of a subject to work upon which not only fed his appetite for romance but demanded research and extensive investigation. The subject was the ballad literature of the Scottish Border. He had already, in boyhood, made acquaintance with Percy's *Reliques*, a collection which influenced him profoundly, not so much in the way of forming a taste which had already a strong bias towards popular poetry, as in giving it respectability and the sanction of a scholarly name. It is very possible that, but for the *Reliques*, *The Minstrelsy of the Scottish Border* would never have been collected and written. About the importance of the service Scott thus did to literature there can be no doubt. His methods may in some respects be challenged. He did not scruple to collate versions, nor to add or amend; and consequently it is not always possible to be sure that what he gives is the authentic traditionary version. Nevertheless, the debt which the student of ballad poetry owes to him is incalculable. He was not only himself an untiring investigator both of MSS. and of oral tradition, but he had the capacity of rousing others to enthusiasm in the service. The *Minstrelsy* is a collection which no man could have brought together without many and willing assistants, and in which few could have enlisted those assistants so successfully as Scott.

But besides the great intrinsic merit of the *Minstrelsy* as a collection of ballads, it has a special significance in the history of Scott. His task as editor not only confirmed his literary tastes, but also gave him an admirable training for the original work of the future. It gave him that knowledge, at once wide and minute, of Border life and character which has never since been equalled, hardly even rivalled. The original ballads which he composed in imitation of the ancient models, either for the *Minstrelsy* or independently, gave him the practice in composition and versification which was desirable as a preliminary to a bolder and longer flight. Not that Scott's ballads are to be regarded as inferior in quality to his more ambitious poems. On the contrary, from *Glenfinlas* and the *Eve of St. John* and *Cadyow Castle* to the ballad of *Harlaw*, written when he had ceased to write verse readily, many of his happiest pictures and touches are to be found in ballads. It would be difficult to point to anything finer of its kind than the picture in *Cadyow Castle* of the murder of Regent Murray. Much of what is most characteristic and best in Scott's verse is exemplified in these few stanzas—his fire and rapidity and vividness, his wealth of historical detail, his mastery of proper names. And in these ballad compositions the judgment of the author is as conspicuous as his genius. Modern ballad writers have as a rule fallen into one of two mistakes. They have either imitated slavishly the ancient models, and proved once again the impossibility of recalling unchanged a past form of art; or, by over-loading the simple structure of popular poetry with modern sentiment and reflection, they have missed its characteristic charm. Scott steered a middle course. Master as he was to an unequalled degree of the diction and turns of thought of the ballad writers, he made no serious and sustained attempt to speak their language. His aim was not to produce identical but similar effects; and while he moulded his verse on the old popular poetry he freely admitted the changes which time had made necessary. None could play the part of an imitator better than Scott when he chose; but the following frankly modern verses from *Cadyow Castle* may be taken to represent his ballad work at the best:—

> "Dark Morton, girt with many a spear,
>   Murder's foul minion, led the van;
> And clash'd their broadswords in the rear
>   The wild Macfarlanes' plaided clan.
>
> "Glencairn and stout Parkhead were nigh,
>   Obsequious at their Regent's rein,
> And haggard Lindsay's iron eye,
>   That saw fair Mary weep in vain.
>
> "'Mid pennon'd spears, a steely grove,
>   Proud Murray's plumage floated high;
> Scarce could his trampling charger move,
>   So close the minions crowded nigh.
>
> "From the rais'd vizor's shade, his eye,
>   Dark-rolling, glanced the ranks along,
> And his steel truncheon, waved on high,
>   Seem'd marshalling the iron throng.
>
> "But yet his sadden'd brow confess'd
>   A passing shade of doubt and awe;
> Some fiend was whispering in his breast,
>   'Beware of injured Bothwellhaugh!'
>
> "The death-shot parts—the charger springs—
>   Wild rises tumult's startling roar!
> And Murray's plumy helmet rings—
>   Rings on the ground, to rise no more."

The success of the *Minstrelsy* gave Scott a position as a man of letters, and the gradual failure of his hopes of professional eminence helped to fix his thoughts upon the new career opening before him. His appointment in 1799 as Sheriff of Selkirkshire, as it furnished the nucleus of an income, rendered him more careless of the drudgery of the Parliament House; and for some years before his appointment in 1806 as one of the principal Clerks of Session (without immediate emolument), he may be regarded as having withdrawn from the competitive work of his profession. In the meantime his edition of the romance of *Sir Tristrem*, a number of contributions to the *Edinburgh Review*, which had been just recently started, and some minor productions, testified, as well as the *Minstrelsy*, to his literary activity. Further, he had already in hand the poem which ultimately received the name of *The Lay of the Last Minstrel*. It was begun in the autumn of 1802, and was originally intended to form part of the third volume of the *Minstrelsy*, but swelled to such a bulk as to require separate publication. Three years passed before it appeared. The enthusiasm with which it was received is well known. The more sober judgment of posterity has also been given; and neither the merits nor the faults of Scott are of such a recondite description that much change need be expected in the critical verdict.

The story of the origin of the *Lay* has been told by Scott himself. The first suggestion came from the Countess of Dalkeith, who wanted a ballad on the Border legend of Gilpin Horner. The kick of a horse, by confining Scott for a few days to his room, gave him leisure to expand the ballad into the first canto of a poem. The finished poem bears marks of the accidental character of its origin. It is loosely constructed; and the part of the Goblin Page in particular, though it has found defenders, is generally, and probably with justice, condemned as unworthy of the poem.   In truth, the whole of the supernatural element, with the exception of the opening of the wizard's grave, is weak and ineffective. As a restorer of romance, Scott was right in giving the supernatural a place in his work; and it may be pleaded that the supernatural of popular poetry is, like Scott's, of a somewhat materialistic and mundane character.   But the elves and fairies, the ghosts and corpse-lights of the ballads produce in their proper context a very different effect from Scott's mischievous page, his feeble mountain spirit and river spirit, or the poor spells of the Ladye of Branksome.   It must be reiterated that the business of a restorer is not to repeat what has been done before, but to produce similar effects by adapting the old to time and circumstance.   Here for once Scott's tact has forsaken him.   He introduces changes indeed into the old supernatural—no ballad-maker ever imagined such spirits as the spirits of mountain and river—but they are changes which enfeeble and emasculate.

But in the case of Scott, more than of most men, it is unprofitable to dwell on shortcomings.   His very excellences are bound up with his defects.   "I am sensible," he wrote long afterwards, "that if there be anything good about my poetry or prose either, it is a hurried frankness of composition, which pleases soldiers, sailors, and young people of bold and active dispositions"; and no wiser word of criticism has ever been written upon him.   But this "hurried frankness" is hardly to be reconciled with care of construction any more than with delicate beauties of language. Scott learnt afterwards to avoid the more obvious faults; but in his first great effort he had not the practice which partly dispenses with the need of care. Notwithstanding great and obvious defects however, the *Lay* was a contribution to the reviving poetry of romance by far the most worthy, in its own line, that had yet appeared. *The Ancient Mariner*, of much higher poetic merit, is too dissimilar to come into comparison. *Christabel*, from which Scott borrowed the idea of the measure, but to which his indebtedness has been frequently exaggerated, was still in MS. Scott was the first man of real genius who successfully attempted romantic narrative; and the wide popularity he achieved was partly due to priority in the field. It was still more due however to merit. He was not only the first in his own peculiar domain, but he remained the best. Byron in his early narrative poems followed Scott's lead; and in the popular judgment the scholar beat the master. But few of those who most heartily admire Byron, and who most warmly assert his superiority to Scott in poetry, will base his reputation upon the narrative poems in which he follows the author of the *Lay*. There is much tinsel in Byron's narrative; Scott's, whatever its defects otherwise, is always genuine.

The *Lay* was remarkable, in the first place, for the energy of the verse, and for the vividness and power with which the author portrayed a wild and stirring life. But it proved also that there had at last arisen a man who could translate history into poetry. Nothing is finer in Scott, nothing more characteristic, than the way in which he utilised the facts of history to heighten the sentiment of his verse :—

"Full many a scutcheon and banner riven,
Shook in the cold night-wind of heaven,
    Around the screened altar's pale ;
And there the dying lamps did burn,
Before thy low and lonely urn,
O gallant Chief of Otterbourne !
    And thine, dark Knight of Liddesdale !
O fading honours of the dead !
O high ambition, lowly laid ! "

It is to passages like this; or like that in which the course of Teviot through ages of war to a time of peace is contrasted with the darkening "tide of human time," or like the admirable picture of the aged minstrel, that the mind turns in thinking of the *Lay*, more even than to the ride of Deloraine.

But above all the *Lay* indicated the rise of a poet as hostile as Wordsworth, though not as obtrusively so, to the methods hitherto in vogue in poetry. It is a singular fate which has made Scott, Tory in politics and worshipper of the past, in spite of himself a revolutionist in literature. It is true, he held no theory such as Wordsworth propounded as to the character of the subjects or the diction appropriate to poetry. On the contrary, he was driven by a kind of intellectual necessity to the choice of subjects remote from ordinary life; and if his general style was simple, the simplicity was not due to critical acquiescence in Wordsworth's doctrine. There is in Scott, as well as in eighteenth century poetry, a kind of conventionality; but the one is the conventionality of romance, the other of classicism. Scott's mosstroopers are not, nor were they intended to be, a picture of the real Borderers of the sixteenth century.

It is only in such passages as that which describes the
approach of Watt Tinlinn, where he is founding directly
on the ballads, that he verges upon realism.   And it is
not merely in the circumstances with which he surrounds
his characters that Scott deviates from literal fact.   Sentiment too is partly conventional.   It is the sentiment of
chivalry grafted on the rude stock of Border manners.
Contrast with anything in Scott Wordsworth's *Song at
the Feast of Brougham Castle.*   In the hands of Scott
noble blood would assert itself, and Clifford would act in
the spirit of the minstrel's song.   Wordsworth, on the
contrary, accepts and, as it were, consecrates the fact that
training more than descent would form him.   But this
element of conventionality does not bring Scott any
nearer to the models of the eighteenth century.   In
subject, in measure, in treatment, in almost every essential, he is opposed to them.   What he admires is what
they contemned.   The "light-horseman sort of stanza,"
the careless force and headlong speed of style, the
battles and broils and sudden deaths, are all as foreign
to the school of Pope as it is possible to conceive.

The success of the *Lay* confirmed Scott in his literary
bent and embarked him upon a poetical career which
continued for about eight years.   He was, it is true, during
those years much more than a writer of poems.   Not to
speak of his professional duties, which were always con-
scientiously discharged, he wrote articles and edited
works to an extraordinary extent.   But even the vol-
uminous editions of Dryden and Swift, which would
have filled so much of most lives, are mere episodes in
that of Scott.   Further, in the very year of the publica-

tion of the *Lay*, he was on the point of attempting a prose romance; but the change in the course of Scott's life was postponed by the unfavourable opinion of the critical friend to whom the early chapters of *Waverley* were submitted. He was still so far from regarding poetry as his business, that, in a letter to Ellis after the publication of the *Lay*, he disclaims any intention of making another serious effort in verse, "unless I should by some strange accident reside so long in the Highlands, and make myself master of their ancient manners, so as to paint them with some degree of accuracy in a kind of *companion* to the Minstrel Lay."[1] A little later however the great popularity of the *Lay* caused him to change his mind. In November, 1806, he was already engaged upon *Marmion*, and it appeared in February, 1808.

There has been a pretty general consensus of critical opinion in favour of this poem as the best that Scott ever wrote. The wonder is, not that this should be the common judgment, but that there should have been so much of hesitancy in pronouncing it. A very large number of those who prefer *Marmion* nevertheless rank it but a little way before the *Lay*. Jeffrey, the chief of contemporary critics, declared it to be "rather clearer that it had greater faults than that it had greater beauties," though he was inclined to believe that it had both. As regards the faults, there are two which are perhaps more conspicuous than any that mark the *Lay*. These are the want of connexion between the introductions to the cantos and the story itself, and the stain upon the character of the central figure. There is artistically no defence for the introductory

---

[1] Lockhart, ii. 51.

epistles. They interrupt the flow of the narrative. They are simply independent poems bound together in the same volume with the Tale of Flodden Field. But just for this reason the fault is of little consequence. It is easy to read the introductions before or after the narrative; and then the story of Marmion stands out clear, distinct, and continuous. The *Lay* contains no violation so flagrant of the law of unity; but the story of the Goblin Page is in truth a far more serious blemish, because it affects the very fabric of the poem.

The forgery by Marmion is not to be so lightly treated. Byron, in the *English Bards and Scotch Reviewers*, justly criticised the hero, "now forging scrolls, now foremost in the fight." That Scott, of all men, with his lofty notions of the influence of high descent and of chivalric ideals, should have fallen into such an error, is astonishing. There is no sufficient reason why the central character of a work of art should not be at once a villain and the technical hero; but the villainy ought to be great and bold, not mean and contemptible. Scott himself was afterwards fully sensible of his error, but, having published the poem, he determined to let it stand. This is one of the instances, comparatively few in number, to which those can point who have censured him for sacrificing his art to his hurry to come before the public. The defence which he made for himself in the epistle to Erskine prefixed to canto iii., and which he repeated and amplified in the course of his career as a novelist, was probably in the main sound. The haste which would have been ruinous to most men suited him. "The works and passages in which I have succeeded," says he in the introduction to *The Fortunes of Nigel*, "have uniformly been written with the greatest rapidity; and when I have seen some of these placed in opposition with others, and commended as more highly finished, I could appeal to pen and standish, that the parts in which I have come feebly off, were much the more laboured."

But when full allowance has been made for these blemishes, and moreover for the fact that there is nothing at all in *Marmion* to set against the singularly felicitous conception of the aged minstrel, nor even against the fine apostrophes put into his mouth at the opening of some of the cantos, it nevertheless seems clear that *Marmion*, so much more firmly knit, so much stronger both in conception and execution, ought to rank above the earlier poem. The narrative is powerful, rapid, and absorbing. There is a good deal that is second rate, parts even that are quite commonplace; but there are more passages and longer passages of high merit than are to be found anywhere else in Scott's poetry. The canto on Flodden has been called "the finest battle-piece since Homer," and probably deserves the praise. "There are few men," it has been said, "who have not at some time or other thought the worse of themselves that they are not soldiers"; and no one perhaps of all who have shared this feeling has read the last canto of *Marmion* without a quickened pulse and a heightened colour. The "hurried frankness" is here exactly suited to the subject, and it rises in dignity with the greatness of the theme.

But though the description of the battle is the longest, it is by no means the only passage of high excellence in *Marmion*. There is much admirable verse in the second canto. The description of Edinburgh as seen from Blackford Hill is justly celebrated as perhaps the best poetical picture Scott ever drew; and the character of Sir David Lindsay is in another way only less admirable.

The introductory epistles, though out of place where they stand, are, when viewed in their true light as independent poems, admirable. They extend collectively to about 1,500 lines; and probably nowhere in Scott will there be found within an equal space so much that is good mingled with so little dross. They have moreover the peculiar interest which attaches to the autobiographical fragments of genius; an interest enhanced by the fact, proved not only by the epistles themselves, but by the fragment prefixed to Lockhart's biography, and by the *Journal* recently published, that Scott could when he wished be one of the most frank and charming of autobiographers. In the present case he speaks with all the warmth and openness of intimacy and affection to six of his dearest friends. These epistles in fact give him a place in another style of poetry than that which he commonly cultivated, a fact obscured only by their arbitrary association with *Marmion*.

From the publication of *Marmion* Scott's career in poetry was a downward one. Between the years 1810-15 he issued five poems of considerable length, three of them on a scale and on a plan similar to those of the two earlier tales; the other two, *The Bridal of Triermain* and *The Vision of Don Roderick*, shorter and different in style and purpose. After 1815, with the unimportant exception of *Harold the Dauntless*, Scott wrote no long piece. He himself explained his abandonment of poetry by reference to the superior popularity and success of Byron; and doubtless that was the immediate cause of the change in his literary career. But there was a deeper cause at work. Scott seems to have exhausted his poetic vein. It is difficult otherwise to understand how it comes that, at a time when his mind ought to have been, and when his own works in prose prove that it was, at its best and brightest; when years had added strength without yet withdrawing the glow and fire of youth, his poetry should exhibit the indubitable marks of decay. In *The Lady of the Lake* the decline was not conspicuous to the author's contemporaries; on the contrary, Jeffrey was inclined to prefer it to his former works; and the demand for it, surpassing that for either of its predecessors, proved the public to be with him. The reason doubtless was that, as a mere story, the *Lady* is perhaps the best of Scott's poems. It excels also in scenic interest. The meeting and blending of Lowlands and Highlands, both in scenery and character, affords unrivalled opportunities for the picturesque. It came besides more nearly home to the popular imagination; for, though the date of the story is earlier than that of the *Lay*, the Highland clan system had so long survived the mosstroopers, as well as the feudal knights of *Marmion*, that the tale appealed to readers as something comparatively close to their own experience. For these reasons, among others, the *Lady* is to this day more often referred to, and probably more often read, than any other of Scott's poems. Nevertheless, its intrinsic merits are far lower than those of *Marmion*, and considerably lower than those of the *Lay.* The author is less master of his subject than he is in his first poem; the subject itself is less grand and massive than that of *Marmion.* Much, too, is written *ad captandum populum.* Of the secret of the king's identity Scott in his introduction of 1830 says: "I relied on it with the same hope of producing effect with which the Irish postboy is said to reserve a 'trot for the avenue.'" Too much of this aiming at effect is evident throughout the poem. Taine, in the course of an extremely shallow and unjust criticism, makes unreality, a desire for mere effect, his gravest charge against Scott. "He is in history, as he is at Abbotsford, bent on arranging points of view and Gothic halls. The moon will come in well there between the towers; here is a nicely placed breastplate, the ray of light which it throws back is pleasant to see on these old hangings; suppose we took out the feudal garments from the wardrobe and invited the guests to a masquerade."[1] This criticism, essentially untrue of Scott in general, finds more justification in *The Lady of the Lake* than in any other of his works. The love-story, always weak in Scott's poems, but more conspicuously so in Ellen than in Clare or Margaret; the stagey figure of the banished Douglas; the Harper, faint reflection of the Last Minstrel;—all these elements and more are meant to captivate the multitude. There are fine scattered passages. The Chase is splendidly fresh and vigorous, the best part unquestionably of the poem; and the battle has a large share of the fire and greatness which Scott never failed to impart to the clash of men in mortal strife. But the highest point of

[1] *History of English Literature,* translated by H. Van Laun, iii. 434.

The Lady of the Lake is below the highest point of *Marmion*.

The Lady of the Lake was the last poem by Scott that was received with full popular favour. The decline in his poetic power became manifest to ordinary readers in *Rokeby* and *The Lord of the Isles*. The falling off in popularity was not more than was justified by the difference in workmanship between these poems and *Marmion ;* but it was a good deal more than the difference between them and *The Lady of the Lake* warranted. Something no doubt was due, as Scott always thought, to the fact that in the interval had come the morning when Byron "awoke and found himself famous." Still more perhaps was due to the fact that the public ear had become accustomed to, and perhaps a trifle weary of Scott's verse, and more critical of its defects. Both these poems, like their immediate predecessor, contain passages not unworthy of the author at his best ; but both as a whole fail to reach a high level. In *The Lord of the Isles* the description of Bannockburn must be regarded as a companion picture to Flodden; but, though good, is clearly inferior to that magnificent battle piece. In *Rokeby*, which of all Scott's poems has had least justice done to it—which some might say is the only one that has not been overpraised —the story is less attractive to the fancy; but it is powerfully told, and in the somewhat monotonous verse there are at least a few great passages. Charles Reade has happily quoted one of these as illustrative of that insight into character which was afterwards displayed by the novelist. When Bertram is meditating the murder of Mortham, it is the memory of benefits he has conferred,

not of those he has received, that almost stays his
hand :—

> " I heard, and thought how, side by side,
>   We two had turn'd the battle's tide,
>   In many a well-debated field,
>   Where Bertram's breast was Philip's shield.
>   I thought on Darien's deserts pale,
>   Where death bestrides the evening gale ;
>   How o'er my friend my cloak I threw,
>   And fenceless faced the deadly dew ;
>   I thought on Quariana's cliff,
>   Where, rescued from our foundering skiff,
>   Through the white breakers' wrath I bore
>   Exhausted Mortham to the shore ;
>   And when his side an arrow found,
>   I suck'd the Indian's venom'd wound.
>   These thoughts like torrents rush'd along,
>   To sweep away my purpose strong."

It is worthy of note that in *Rokeby* Scott gives the most
convincing proof of his lyrical power.   There are a few
fine lyrics in the earlier poems, as for example the *Coro-
nach* in *The Lady of the Lake* ; but the songs of *Rokeby*
are on the whole superior to those of any of the other
poems.   "Brignall banks are wild and fair" is a beautiful
piece ; and the following is more beautiful still :—

> " ' A weary lot is thine, fair maid,
>   A weary lot is thine !
>   To pull the thorn thy brow to braid,
>   And press the rue for wine !
>   A lightsome eye, a soldier's mien,
>   A feather of the blue,
>   A doublet of the Lincoln green,—
>   No more of me you knew,
>   My love !
>   No more of me you knew.

" ' This morn is merry June, I trow,
  The rose is budding fain;
But she shall bloom in winter's snow,
  Ere we two meet again.'
He turn'd his charger as he spake,
  Upon the river shore,
He gave his bridal reins a shake,
  Said, ' Adieu for evermore,
        My love !
And adieu for evermore.' "

The lyric was the only strain of poetry which Scott
retained in after years. He enriched his novels with
verse of a quality to prove to all capable of judging
that the Great Unknown was a poet of no mean order.
In these lyrics there is a fineness of touch hardly to
be expected of their author. In the songs of Meg
Merrilies, *Twist ye, twine ye,* and *Wasted, weary,*
wherefore stay ; in the *Serenade Song* and other scraps
of verse in *The Pirate;* in the lines on *Time* in *The*
Antiquary; in many an original fragment prefixed to
his chapters when invention proved easier than recol-
lection; and in occasional verses like the exquisite
lines beginning "The sun upon the Weirdlaw Hill,"
we have proof that Scott was, when he pleased, as much
master of the minute touch as of the broad bold strokes
of the painter of Flodden Field. It cannot however
be matter of regret that, after 1815, his verses were,
with the exception of *Harold the Dauntless*, only occasional.
He could never have stood in the first rank of poetry.
He had given the world all or nearly all he had to give
in the way of versified romance; and, unknown to himself, a far greater career was on the point of opening to
him.

But before the change in his literary career took place there had been a change in his life which demands notice, because it is very intimately related to the subsequent course of his writings. Those connexions also had meanwhile been formed which governed his life to its close.

Scott married in 1797. His first home was a modest cottage at Lasswade. Thence he removed in 1804 to Ashestiel, near Selkirk; and strangely enough he made the "flitting" unwillingly, in compliance with pressure put upon him by the Lord Lieutenant of Selkirkshire, that he might conform to a law requiring a sheriff to reside at least four months in the year within the bounds of his jurisdiction. But the change which made him a resident in his own Borderland, the home from infancy of his imagination, was too congenial to be long regarded as a disagreeable necessity. Years afterwards he said to Washington Irving, "When I have been for some time in the rich scenery about Edinburgh, which is like ornamented garden land, I begin to wish myself back again among my own honest grey hills; and if I did not see the heather, at least once a year, *I think I should die.*"[1] About the same time, what between literary profits, professional income, and the bequest of his uncle, Captain Robert Scott, his worldly circumstances were very much improved. Lockhart calculates that, independent of the proceeds of literature and other uncertain sources of wealth, Scott was now in receipt of a fixed income of about £1000 a year, to which was added in 1806 the pro-

[1] Irving, quoted by Lockhart, iv. 92.

spect of an ultimate £800 more from the Clerkship of Session. With increase of means came naturally enlarged notions of living; but, what proved to be more important than any increase of his own expenses, the possession of his uncle's legacy, which Scott had originally intended to invest in the purchase of land, tempted him to embark in commercial enterprise. Some years before an old schoolfellow, James Ballantyne, had started business as a printer. He was encouraged and assisted by Scott, and the business grew till it was too large for his capital. He approached his old companion, to whom he was already indebted, with a request for another loan. Scott answered that he could not advance more by way of loan, but was willing to embark a suitable amount of capital to purchase a third share of the business. Thus was formed the connexion of all others the most influential upon Scott's career, the source of his darkest troubles, but the spring also of his most strenuous and successful exertions. "Its effects," says Lockhart, "were in truth so mixed and balanced during the vicissitudes of a long and vigorous career, that I at this moment doubt whether it ought, on the whole, to be considered with more of satisfaction or of regret." This partnership was entered into in 1805. In 1809 Scott involved himself in commerce still further, and most disastrously, by the establishment of a new house, John Ballantyne & Co., booksellers, of which he was also partner. The head of this firm, a brother of James Ballantyne, was a man destitute alike of capital and character; and nothing in Scott's career is more surprising than his willingness to associate himself so intimately with such a person. A quarrel with the great Edinburgh publisher, Constable, tempted him to start this second firm. It was unfortunate from the beginning; managed as it was by John Ballantyne it could not be otherwise. Scott himself was much to blame; for no small share of the embarrassments of the firm was due to injudicious recommendations by him. But he had deep reason to complain of the concealments and evasions of his principal partner, who habitually neglected to make timely provision for the calls which he knew or should have known were impending upon them. The troubles came to a crisis in 1813, when Scott had a foretaste of the bitterness of the doom which awaited him at a later day, and when a crash was only averted by the assistance of the Duke of Buccleuch and of the once hostile but now friendly house of Constable. This may be considered the end of the publishing house of Ballantyne; but the entanglements it had woven round him long continued to fetter Scott.

During these same years Scott was gradually entering upon the life by which he is himself best known. His first purchase of land was made in 1811. The farm between Melrose and Selkirk which he bought was then known by the name of the Clarty (*i.e.* Dirty) Hole; but he rechristened it from the neighbouring passage of the Tweed by the now famous title of Abbotsford. In the following year he removed from Ashestiel to his new home; and for many a day he was full of plans for building and for the purchase and improvement of land, until by the union of small properties whose owners he bought out, he created an estate. At the same time, by the gradual enlargement of his originally modest plans for building, he reared the castle with which his name is more intimately associated than perhaps the name of any other English man of letters has ever been with the place in which he lived.

With Scott's efforts to consolidate the estate and build the mansion of Abbotsford are connected some of the chief problems regarding his character. Money was required to gratify these desires. It was required also in connexion with his still unavowed commercial ventures. The consequence is that money matters fill a large portion of his life, and that his character has been in this point much misread. There was a time, as Mr. Ruskin points out, when good people looked upon Scott, Burns, and Byron as the world, the flesh, and the devil. Worldliness has thus been considered the keynote of his character; and he has been charged with a love of money, unworthy in any man, but a hundred times unworthy in one so gifted. It would be untrue to say that there is no foundation for the charge. Lockhart, scrupulously fair, though deeply attached to the memory of Scott, says, "I dare not deny that he set more of his affections, during great part of his life, upon worldly things, wealth among others, than might have become such an intellect."[1] But to regard him as a mere vulgar money-lover is a profound mistake. Scott's appetite for wealth was intimately connected with the higher dreams of his imagination. He lived in the ideal world of old romance so long that he was mastered by the desire to realise his visions. He was to be the founder of a family, and Abbotsford its seat. The almost unbounded hospitality exercised there for years was quite

[1] vi. 98.

in keeping with the part which the owner aspired to play.   His ambition was no doubt a mistaken, but it was far from a vulgar one.   It was, on the contrary, peculiarly fitted to his imaginative character.   Abbotsford was a "romance in stone and lime," in a sense not thought of by the man who merely regards its architecture.

The removal from Ashestiel took place in 1812.   Scott's poetic period was already near its close.   It has been mentioned that he wrote the introductory chapters to *Waverley* as early as 1805.   He submitted those chapters to William Erskine, the friend on whose critical judgment he chiefly relied.   The verdict was so unfavourable that Scott was induced to drop the project; but as Erskine founded only on the portion which precedes the hero's departure for Scotland, his condemnation of a work afterwards so successful reflects no great discredit on his literary taste.   In 1810 Scott appears to have turned again to this old fragment; for Lockhart prints a letter of that year from James Ballantyne with reference to it. Without pronouncing an absolute condemnation, Ballantyne spoke so coldly that Scott once more threw it aside. Finally, in 1813, in rummaging an old cabinet in search of fishing tackle, he came upon the half-forgotten fragment, and determined to finish it.   The completed novel of *Waverley* was published in 1814.   Its brilliant and immediate success determined Scott's literary course for the rest of his life.   *Waverley* was the first of a great series of novels which, taken all in all, are unparalleled in the annals of English fiction.   It is questionable whether any man ever wrote so much upon whose time so many claims— legal, social, and miscellaneous—were made and met;

though, if productiveness be measured merely by the quantity written, smaller men have in this respect surpassed Scott. There have been others who in the judgment of some, though this is more questionable, have equalled and even excelled Scott's best work. But in the combination of quantity with high quality, Scott stands alone among the great writers of English fiction.

It has been customary to assert that Scott's best novels were all produced within a few years of *Waverley*, and that there is manifest afterwards a great falling off. Mr. Ruskin, though he admits that Scott produced great work afterwards, draws a sharp line at the severe illness from which Scott suffered in 1819, and ranks six of the seven novels written previous to that date above all else their author ever produced. The six novels thus preferred above the rest are—*Waverley, Guy Mannering, The Antiquary, Old Mortality, Rob Roy,* and *The Heart of Midlothian.* It would certainly be impossible to name among Scott's subsequent works another half dozen fit to stand beside these; and the balance of critical opinion inclines to finding three of the six—namely, *Guy Mannering, The Antiquary,* and *Old Mortality*—the greatest of all his writings. But for its feeble close *The Heart of Midlothian* would have made a fourth, perhaps the greatest of all. It is therefore true that the average of Scott's work in the later period is lower than that of these opening years. But to say nothing of the chivalric glow and elevation of *Ivanhoe,* the mental decay which admitted of the production of *The Fortunes of Nigel* and *Quentin Durward* was by no means great; and the classification which ranks these as decidedly inferior to *Rob Roy* is open to serious question.   The truth seems to be, not that Scott's intellect failed, but that he used up for his earlier fictions the material best suited to his imagination.   In later days he attempted subjects, such as *St. Ronan's Well*, which had little attraction for him; but down at least to 1828, when *The Fair Maid of Perth* was published, though there were occasional failures, there was nothing that seems really to indicate decay.   In *Count Robert of Paris* and *Castle Dangerous* it is painfully manifest.

For fourteen years therefore after the publication of *Waverley*, not for five only, Scott continued to produce work which deserves to be called great.   In that period he wrote considerably over twenty works of fiction, mostly of three-volume length, though some few are comparatively short.   These novels exhibit a range of power for which the poems hardly prepare the reader.   The same qualities, both merits and defects, that we find in the verse are indeed present in the prose.   One of the best criticisms of Scott, the *Letters of J. L. Adolphus*, was written to prove from internal evidence that the author of the poems avowed by Scott and the then nameless author of the Waverley Novels must be one and the same person; and the argument is as conclusive as an argument founded upon internal evidence can well be.   But the highest qualities of the novels are without any proper parallel in the poems.   The characters are drawn at once with bolder and subtler strokes than Scott ever displayed in verse—than perhaps the conditions of narrative poetry permitted.

Classifications of a man's works are often, perhaps as a rule, of little value; and if pushed beyond due limits they may easily become worse than useless. It will nevertheless be convenient to range Scott's novels under different heads. One of the most obvious lines of division is that which separates the historical novels from those of which the scene is laid in the writer's own day or very near it. Another is the division between those of which the scene is laid in Scotland, or better, of which the leading characters are Scotch, and those which relate the adventures of men and women of other countries.

A distinction is sometimes drawn between historical novels and novels of manners. The term "historical novel" may obviously be used in more senses than one. It may denote a work of fiction the main incidents of which are historical facts, and the actors all or chiefly historical personages. In this sense a considerable number of the plays of Shakespeare are historical dramas. He no doubt has taken liberties with history; but though the sober historian, whose first business is with fact, would not follow the dramatist, he would name and characterise the same personages and narrate the same leading events. If however any of Scott's novels be called historical, they are not so in this sense. *Waverley, Old Mortality, Quentin Durward, Ivanhoe, Kenilworth, The Abbot, The Monastery,* and others, number among their characters names known to history, and bring before the reader events which have actually happened. But in every case there is so great an admixture of characters and incidents purely fictitious, as essentially to modify the sense in which they are to be called historical. The novels above named and others may however be fairly looked upon as pictures of the state of society in different ages and countries. As such they fully satisfied Scott's contemporaries. They have since been attacked as inaccurate and misleading. One critic complains that costumes, scenery, externals alone are exact; another asserts that these very externals are untrustworthy, and finds his enjoyment of the Waverley Novels destroyed because the cut of the hero's coat is not according to the highest fashion of his age. The critic has not yet been found—at least since Shakespeare's fame was established beyond question—so sensitive to violations of history as to be altogether alienated by the description of Imogen's chamber in a British palace about the beginning of the Christian era. All the charges against Scott which have been mentioned are probably true. Few men have a knowledge of history equal to that of Scott; and his was not only a wide and general knowledge, but one which descended at many points to curiously minute detail. But he wrote rapidly, aimed at producing broad effects, and trusted to a memory which, though marvellously tenacious, no doubt frequently deceived him. Besides, he invented freely where memory failed to furnish him with material. It may then well be that all the censures passed upon him for inaccuracy are merited; but they are unimportant.[1]

---

[1] The fallaciousness of this "minute criticism" could not be better exposed than in a passage in Mr. Nichol's recently published monograph on Carlyle:—"Applying this minute criticism to *The French Revolution,* one reviewer has found that the author has given the wrong number to a regiment: another esteemed scholar has discovered that there are seven errors in the famous account of the flight to Varennes, to wit:—the delay in the departure was due to Bouillé, not to the Queen; she did not lose her way and so delay the start; Ste. Menehould is too big to be called a village; on the arrest, it was the Queen, not the King, who asked for hot water and

The objection of those who urge that language, sentiment, and characters are essentially modern, seems more
serious than the rather frivolous critical antiquarianism
which takes exception to the colour of a ribbon or the
shape of a bonnet ; and even those who make no pretensions to profound historical lore can easily see that,
whatever it is worth, the objection is, at least to a considerable extent, true.   In none of his works does Scott
succeed in presenting, it may be added that he never
seriously attempts to present, such a masterly reproduction of a past style as Thackeray's *Esmond*.   The language
of Cedric the Saxon, of Wamba the jester, and of Gurth
the swineherd, is certainly not the language of Saxon
England in the reign of Cœur de Lion ; and if the
nobler ideals of the days of chivalry are given with spirit
and effect, its meaner side is almost entirely concealed.
Scott knew the fact as well as any of his critics.   There
is fortunately one of his imaginative works which can be
brought into direct comparison with a work of research
describing the same district and period.   *The Lay of the
Last Minstrel* gives the poet's representation of the society
which Scott attempted to describe and illustrate as a
historian in his *Border Minstrelsy*.   The difference proves
that, whether Scott was right or wrong in altering history

eggs; the coach went rather faster than is stated; and, above all,
infandum! it was not painted yellow, but green and black.   This
criticism does not in any degree detract from the value of one of the
most vivid and substantially accurate narratives in the range of
European literature.   Carlyle's object was to convey the soul of the
Revolution, not to register its upholstery.   The annalist, be he dry-
asdust or gossip, is, in legal phrase, 'the devil' of the prose artist,
whose work makes almost as great a demand on the imaginative
faculty as that of the poet."

for the purposes of his art, he did so deliberately. As the intellectual heir of the old romancers he could not well do otherwise. And unless art is to be resolved into imitation, and bound down to copy fact, it is hard to see wherein lies the great error. The historical accuracy of his pictures of Graham of Claverhouse, his Louis XI., his Mary Queen of Scots, and even his King James, may perhaps be challenged : it is more important from the literary point of view to note that they are real human beings. And it will not be easy by any insistence upon errors of detail to shake the conviction of the unsophisticated reader that Scott's remarkable pictures of bygone ages are not only spirited and striking, but in their broad outlines true. The due degree of praise and blame may not have been exactly apportioned by him to the Covenanters and to their opponents, or to the party of Queen Mary and the party of the Reformers ; but a fair reading of contemporary documents would probably convince most students, unless they had prejudged the case, that there were in Scotland, in the latter half of the seventeenth century, enthusiasts capable of all that is ascribed to Burley, and preachers whose style had a strong resemblance to that of the ministers of *Old Mortality*. In *Waverley* again the disorders and dissensions in the army of the Pretender, the self-seeking of some of his followers and the disinterested devotion of others, the general confusion and the fear, are all faithful historical pictures.

Whether it can in any case be profitable to attempt much more than Scott has accomplished may be questioned. Until the present century it can hardly be said that

even the desire existed to represent with fidelity and
accuracy a far distant age. Artists of various kinds did
indeed frequently lay the scene of their works in other
times and countries than their own; but they relied upon
the broad facts of human nature rather than upon the
comparatively minute differences of age and race. The
spirit of their work is shown in pictures like Leonardo's
" Last Supper," with its table appointments, not of the age
of Christ, but of the Renaissance; or in the plays of
Shakespeare founded upon old British history, but repre-
senting manners and characters essentially Elizabethan.
The experience of the last two or three generations
seems to show that, however anachronistic these pictures may
be, the principle at the root of them is artistically sounder
than that which aims at perfect accuracy. For though
the accuracy is in itself highly desirable, in the pursuit
of it freedom and strength, which are much more important, have generally been lost. Thackeray's *Esmond*
stands out as the one conspicuous triumph of the stricter
historical school; and its success is accountable in the
first place by the fact that the age chosen is comparatively near at hand, and secondly by the fact that the
grade of society represented is that which has left the
fullest documents. Scott himself was one of the first who
aimed at a greater degree of accuracy than had previously
contented the world; but his practical good sense limited
the aim to the elimination of anachronisms likely to be
offensive to advancing knowledge. He found in history
a boundless store of material for his imagination; but he
never allowed himself to be cramped by it.

Yet it was not mere caprice or accident which led

Scott to lay the scenes of most of 'his stories in the past. Though in a few cases, conspicuously in *Guy Mannering* and *The Antiquary*, he succeeds to admiration with materials destitute of the charm of distance and in no sense historical, it is plain that he is as a rule happiest when he has the large background of national life to work upon. With characteristic self-depreciation he refers to his own style as "the big bow-wow strain"; and so much is true, that he neither did nor probably could work well on the limited canvas of domestic life. Even in his non-historical novels he loves to introduce elements of excitement foreign to common life—in *Guy Mannering* the smugglers and the gipsies; in *The Antiquary* the alarm of invasion, the perilous adventure of the Mussel-craig, and the gloom and tragedy of the Glenallan family. He is fond too of a supernatural element, and contrives to find a place for it, or for something which produces like effects, in the conjuring of the Oxford student, the incantations of Meg Merrilies, and the German tale translated by Miss Wardour. Scott rightly felt that distance in time was necessary to enable him to introduce such elements as these with full effect into his tales. Whether the historical details, or what is more important, the historical portraits, are reliable or not, by laying his scene in the past he attained artistic effects which could not be produced, or could not be indefinitely repeated, in novels describing contemporary manners.

The great strength of Scott lies, there can be little doubt, in his pictures of Scottish life and character. They are wonderfully varied and rich. He knew his countrymen thoroughly; and, especially in his portraiture of the peasantry and lower ranks, he put his knowledge into language of remarkable felicity. In a passage in *The Fortunes of Nigel* he has himself explained the secret of his success:—"For ourselves, we can assure the reader—and perhaps if we have ever been able to afford him amusement, it is owing in a great degree to this cause—that we never found ourselves in company with the stupidest of all possible companions in a post-chaise, or with the most arrant cumber-corner that ever occupied a place in the mail-coach, without finding, that in the course of our conversation with him, we had some ideas suggested to us, either grave or gay, or some information communicated in the course of our journey, which we should have regretted not to have learned, and which we should be sorry to have immediately forgotten." Lockhart's biography confirms and strengthens what is here said. Scott was able to draw advantage from everybody who came in contact with him; but it was because of the sympathy and kindness he first extended to them. The poacher, Tom Purdie, was converted into his devoted servant. "Sir Walter," remarks someone in Lockhart, "speaks to every man as if they were blood-relations."[1] "He aye did as the lave did," says Shortreed, "never made himself the great man, or took ony airs in the company."[2] These qualities—perfect readiness to throw himself into the life of any company, the power of sympathy which it implied, and the personal charm proved by his capacity to attract to himself men of the most widely different character and social station—were

[1] v. 322.   [2] i. 198.

the means by which he accumulated much of the material he used in his novels. His characters, though not commonly copies of individuals, nearly all contain features he had observed in persons whom he had encountered. Greater reserve on his part, or lack of sympathy, would have prevented others from revealing themselves to him, and impoverished the stores of his observation.

It was his catholic gift of sympathy which enabled Scott to break down the barrier of class distinctions, and thus enriched his novels with those characters of humble life which are on the whole the best of all he has drawn. His pictures of the Scottish peasantry are numerous, varied, almost invariably happy, and in many cases of supreme excellence. Cuddie Headrigg, slow-minded, almost stupid, faithful, brave though cautious, and with some of that gift of dry humour so characteristic of his class, is the Scotch ploughman to the life. He is "no clear if he can pleugh ony place but the Mains and Mucklewhame." He is aware of his own intellectual inferiority to his mother Mause, yet he feels that "for getting a service or getting forward in the warld, he could somegate gar the wee pickle sense he had gang muckle farther than hers, though she could crack like ony minister o' them a'." His obtuseness is partly assumed : "There's whiles convenience in looking a wee stupid." His mother Mause is an admirable contrast, quick where her son is dull, an enthusiast, eager that he should testify and preserve the marriage garment unsullied, one in whom the fervid strain of her country's blood has overpowered the caution and obscured the

shrewdness associated with its cooler side. She is however as true to life as her son. History has again and
again proved that a zeal which when stirred is too hot
to be discriminating, is as much a Scotch characteristic as
"canniness"; and it was his conviction of this fact, and
his consciousness of the danger of excess involved in it,
that made Scott shrink from the political experiments
which the Edinburgh Whigs of his day were never tired
of advocating.

The religion of Mause is heightened to enthusiasm by
the circumstances of the time, and the enthusiasm par-
takes, as it is apt to do, of absurdity; but no picture of
the Scottish lower orders would be complete which did not
recognise as part of their permanent character a religion
quieter, but only needing the call of necessity to blaze
out as intense and strong as in the days of the Covenant.
In Davy Deans a zeal as warm as that of Mause, and
more stern, as becomes his sex, is just touched by post-
revolutionary calm: in his son-in-law, Reuben Butler, a
milder disposition and further lapse of time contribute
still more to soften it. But Scott was too true an artist
to confine the religion of his novels to those characters
in which it is the main ingredient. In the grand old
beggar, Edie Ochiltree, nothing is finer than the strain
of homely divinity with which he on occasion diversifies
and enriches his conversation. He has been a soldier,
and in youth has shared the wildness and excesses of his
profession; but in the evening of his days serious thoughts
come as he wanders by the burnsides. We get some of
the results of his meditations, as well as some insight
into his wilder youth, in his conversation with Lovel in

the ruins of St. Ruth after the duel. "'We will be better here'—said Edie, seating himself on the stone bench, and stretching the lappet of his blue gown upon the spot, when he motioned Lovel to sit down beside him—'We will be better here than doun below—the air's free and mild, and the savour of the wall-flowers, and siccan shrubs as grow on thae ruined wa's, is far mair refreshing than the damp smell doun below yonder. They smell sweetest by night-time thae flowers, and they're maist aye seen about ruined buildings. Now, Maister Lovel, can ony o' you scholars gie a gude reason for that?'

"Lovel replied in the negative.

"'I am thinking,' resumed the beggar, 'that they'll be like mony folks' gude gifts, that often seem maist gracious in adversity—or maybe it's a parable, to teach us no to slight them that are in the darkness of sin and the decay of tribulation, since God sends odours to refresh the mirkest hour, and flowers and pleasant bushes to clothe the ruined buildings. And now I wad like a wise man to tell me whether Heaven is maist pleased wi' the sight we are looking upon—thae pleasant and quiet lang streaks o' moonlight that are lying sae still on the floor o' this auld kirk, and glancing through the great pillars and stanchions o' the carved windows, and just dancing like on the leaves o' the dark ivy as the breath o' wind shakes it—I wonder whether this is mair pleasing to Heaven than when it was lighted up wi' lamps, and candles nae doubt, and roughies, and wi' the mirth and the frankincent that they speak of in the Holy Scripture, and wi' organs assuredly, and men and women singers, and sackbuts, and dulcimers, and a' instruments o' music—I wonder if that was acceptable, or whether it is of these grand parafle o' ceremonies that holy writ says ' It is an abomination to me.' I am thinking, Maister Lovel, if twa puir contrite spirits like yours and mine fand grace to make our petition ' "—— But here he was interrupted in a train of thought not only beautiful in itself, but appropriate alike to the character and the situation. Scott was a man of too much taste to dwell often upon such themes; but he could use them with effect when occasion called; just as, also upon occasion, he could reawaken the spirit and patriotism of the old soldier, beggar though he was:—"' Me no muckle to fight for, sir?'" exclaims Edie when Oldbuck suggests that his "stake in the country" is small—"' is na there the country to fight for, and the burnsides that I gang daundering beside, and the hearths o' the gude-wives that gie me my bit bread, and the bits o' weans that come toddling to play wi' me when I come about a landward town?—De'il,' he continued, grasping his pike-staff with great emphasis, 'an' I had as gude pith as I hae gude-will, and a gude cause, I should gie some o' them a day's kemping.'" To no one perhaps but to Shakespeare or to Scott would it have occurred to make the old beggar, shrewd, sly, humorous, "pawky" in ordinary circumstances, the sharer of thoughts so solemn, so lofty, and so just.

But the ordinary pitch in reference to this class of characters is, as it ought to be, much lower than in the passages quoted. Dry humour is the most notable feature in the character of the Scottish peasantry; and it is this which is most prominent in Scott's stories. The humour

P

is sometimes the property of the character itself, as pre-eminently in Edie Ochiltree, and partly in Cuddie Head-rigg; sometimes it is the creation of the author out of the circumstances in which he places his man, as in the case of the stubborn, conceited, and dogmatical Richie Moniplies, or of Dominie Sampson, who, innocent of all wish to make mirth, is the occasion of much.   The fidelity and lofty disinterestedness of which the Scottish poor are capable is amply acknowledged in Richie, Cuddie, Caleb Balderstone and many others; but so are meanness, self-seeking, hypocrisy, and scant honesty in Andrew Fair-service and Bryce Snailsfoot.   Andrew is one of the best of Scott's characters; and though Bryce is not equal to him, there are some exquisite touches in his portrait, such as his rebuke of Mordaunt when he himself is on the point of plundering the shipwrecked seaman's chest:—
"Dinna swear, sir; dinna swear, sir—I will endure no swearing in my presence; and if you lay a finger on me, that am taking the lawful spoil of the Egyptians, I will give ye a lesson ye shall remember from this day to Yule."

Scott was likewise master of the tragedy and pathos of humble life.   "Ay, ay," said he in the hearing of Lockhart, speaking of Melrose, "if one could look into the heart of that little cluster of cottages, no fear but you would find materials enow for tragedy as well as comedy.   I undertake to say there is some real romance at this moment going on down there, that, if it could have justice done to it, would be well worth all the fiction that was ever spun out of human brains."[1]   It is this

[1] Lockhart, v. 285.

full faith in a proposition to which many give only a half assent, that all humanity is potentially present in its lowliest as well as its highest specimen, which explains Scott's thorough mastery of peasant life. His impressive picture of the Mucklebackets is well known. The whole story of the Deans family, one of the noblest ever told, exhibits the same sympathy. Not quite so famous is the passage of wild but pathetic beauty in which the wandering Meg Merrilies refers to the ruins of her hut :—
" 'Do you see that blackit and broken end of a sheeling ?— There my kettle boiled for forty years—there I bore twelve buirdly sons and daughters—Where are they now ?—Where are the leaves that were on that auld ash-tree at Martinmas !—the west wind has made it bare—and I'm stripped too.—Do you see that saugh tree ?—it's but a blackened rotten stump now—I've sat under it mony a bonnie summer afternoon, when it hung its gay garlands ower the poppling water.—I've sat there, and,' elevating her voice, ' I've held you on my knee, Henry Bertram, and sung ye sangs of the auld barons and their bloody wars.—It will ne'er be green again, and Meg Merrilies will never sing sangs mair, be they blithe or sad. But ye'll no forget her ?— and ye'll gar big up the auld wa's for her sake ?—and let somebody live there that's ower gude to fear them of another world.—For if ever the dead came back amang the living, I'll be seen in this glen mony a night after these crazed banes are in the mould."

The portraits of persons in a higher rank that are strikingly excellent are less numerous; but there are enough of them to show that Scott's power does not desert him here. He is, it is true, happiest as a rule where the character presents some outstanding peculiarity. Such is the case with the antiquarianism of Oldbuck, the pedantic learning of the Baron of Bradwardine, and the mental inconsequence of the far-descended but weak-minded Godfrey Bertram, who ought to be placed beside Mrs. Quickly. It is the case also with King James of *The Fortunes of Nigel*, a portrait hardly less eminent in merit than its original was in position. Most of the details of his manner and character are taken from contemporary documents; but a comparison between the documents in question and Scott's reproduction, and a study of the way in which he has breathed into the dry bones the breath of life, affords the most instructive insight into the workings of creative genius. But there are not wanting figures in the novels destitute of such peculiarities, who nevertheless are as fine as almost any of these. There are several in James's own family. The Prince Charles of *Waverley* is a lively sketch; his ancestress, Queen Mary, is depicted with equal felicity and more elaboration. The Duke of Rothesay, son of Robert III., quick-witted and high spirited, but shallow, debauched, and reckless, is one of the finest characters drawn in Scott's later years. Claverhouse, brave soldier and lofty enthusiast, seeing and owning the resemblance as well as the contrast between himself and the fanatic, Balfour of Burley, is, whether true to history or not, a perfect picture of a gentleman. Fergus MacIvor is a kindred figure, but less elevated and more stained with selfish ambition; in which respect he is finely contrasted with his enthusiastic and disinterested sister Flora. Scott was far too true a gentleman himself to fail in painting gentlemen. He shows a power much subtler than that of giving to a person in his own rank of life the manners and the sentiments which belong to it; his farmers, peasants, and servants, though they are never gifted with an impossible refinement of manner, are, except where the object is to paint a mean or sordid character, gentlemen at heart. One instance must suffice where many might be chosen. In the tragic and pathetic chapter which records the trial and condemnation of Vich Ian Vohr, Evan Dhu, his faithful clansman and foster-brother, pledges himself that if the judge will but pardon his chief, he himself will go to the Highlands and bring six of the best of the clan to suffer in his stead. A brutal laugh arises in court at the extraordinary nature of the proposal. "The judge checked this indecency, and Evan, looking sternly around when the murmur abated, 'If the Saxon gentlemen are laughing,' he said, 'because a poor man, such as me, thinks my life, or the life of six of my degree, is worth that of Vich Ian Vohr, it's like enough they may be very right; but if they laugh because they think I would not keep my word, and come back to redeem him, I can tell them they ken neither the heart of a Hielandman nor the honour of a gentleman.'"

Scott's female characters are unquestionably less excellent than the male characters of his novels. The heroines, like the heroes, are as a rule weak and uninteresting. Yet Rebecca of York is a striking exception; and Jeanie Deans is perhaps the noblest heroine in fiction —poor, plain, commonplace in intellect, but more than redeemed by loftiness of principle and ungrudging self-devotion. Flora and Rose too, the contrasted heroines of *Waverley*, have considerable merit. And where Scott steps out of his own rank of life and feels himself unfettered by the conventionalities of social position, his women are almost as good as his men. It is because Jeanie Deans has not exactly the ordinary position of the heroine that he succeeds so well with her. His subordinate women are frequently admirable. Meg Dods is the ideal keeper of an inn that is no "hottle." Her professional sister, Mrs. M'Candlish, is also excellent. Ailie Dinmont, Alison Wilson, and women of the humbler ranks generally, are admirably drawn.

Characters like Meg Merrilies, Norna, and Madge Wildfire, either wholly or partially insane, are frequently portrayed by Scott. So are weird beings like Elspeth Mucklebacket and the crones who dress the corpse in *The Bride of Lammermoor*. The reason doubtless is that their presence is a sort of gateway for the awful and the supernatural, which can no longer be introduced by the older device of witches. His treatment of insanity is worthy of study. The three first named of these characters are all disordered in intellect, but all differently. The minds of Norna and of Madge are shaken through much the same causes; but the effect upon an intellect originally powerful and a character originally elevated is very different from that upon one "constitutionally unsettled by giddiness and vanity." Norna, though of more importance in the action of the novel, and though theatrically impressive, is much less ably drawn than Madge, whose wild, disjointed volubility, overweening vanity, glimmerings of remorse, and brief moments of prudence, the signs of a "doubtful, uncertain, and twilight sort of rationality," constitute together a picture not easily surpassed. But Meg Merrilies is a creation of higher genius still. Hers is the most complex case of the three. Her derangement is not the result of ordinary causes; nor is it, like Madge's, intensified by original weakness of mind; it is partly the legacy of a wild strain of blood; partly the result of imposture continued till it produced belief in the actor; partly the outcome of a life of hardship, misfortune, and war with society. At her first entrance, there is joviality as well as wildness and enthusiasm in her character. It darkens after the quarrel with the laird of Ellangowan; and age, the loss of her children, and long association with desperate men do the rest. Almost to the end it remains doubtful to onlookers how far she is playing a part, and how far the victim of self-delusion. The veil is lifted to the reader in the closing scenes of her life, her guidance of Bertram to the cave and her deathbed.

I have said that one of the causes of Scott's liking for such characters was probably that they gave a means of introducing the awful and the supernatural. It is remarkable that there is hardly any of his great poems or novels which does not contain at least some hint of agencies beyond the common laws of nature. Doubtless this is partly to be explained by his studies in popular poetry, where such agencies are common; but it points also to a tendency native to his mind. Mr. Hutton views Scott's as a nature unusually free from superstition, and quotes, in illustration of his iron nerve, the story how on one occasion he found himself at an inn where there was no bed unoccupied, except one which stood in a room in which lay a corpse. He first satisfied himself that the

person had not died of any contagious disorder; then
took the other bed, lay down, and never, he says, had a
better night's sleep in his life.   That the man who did
this had strong nerves, and that he could at will shake
himself free from those causeless terrors which beset many
who do not yield a moment's assent to the superstitions
which they seem to imply, requires no demonstration.
But it is by no means so clear that Scott's mind was
wholly uninfluenced by superstition.   A careful reader of
the biography will probably come to the conclusion that
Lockhart was of a different opinion.   The story of " Laird
Nippy," which Lockhart relates with its appropriate com-
ment by Scott before and after the bankruptcy which
brought long-foretold destruction on his family, is suggestive.   The Laidlaws of the neighbourhood of Ashestiel,
of whom " Laird Nippy " was one, " traced their descent,
in the ninth degree, to an ancestress who, in the days of
John Knox, fell into trouble from a suspicion of witch-
craft.   In her time the Laidlaws were rich and prosperous,
and held rank among the best gentry of Tweeddale; but
in some evil hour, her husband, the head of his blood,
reproached her with her addiction to the black art, and
she, in her anger, cursed the name and lineage of Laidlaw.
Her only son, who stood by, implored her to revoke
the malediction; but in vain.   Next day, however, on the
renewal of his entreaties, she carried him with her into the
woods, made him slay a heifer, sacrificed it to the power
of evil in his presence, and then, collecting the ashes in
her apron, invited the youth to see her commit them to
the river.   'Follow them,' said she, 'from stream to pool
as long as they float visible, and as many streams as you

shall then have passed, for so many generations shall your descendants prosper. After that they shall, like the rest of the name, be poor, and take their part in my curse.' The streams he counted, were nine; 'and now,' Scott would say, 'look round you in this country, and sure enough the Laidlaws are one and all landless men, with the single exception of Auld Nippy.' Many times had I heard both him and William Laidlaw tell this story, before any suspicion got abroad that Nippy's wealth rested on insecure foundations. Year after year, we never escorted a stranger by the Peel, but I heard the tale;—and at last it came with a new conclusion;—'and now, think whatever we choose of it, my good friend Nippy is a bankrupt.'"[1] And Lockhart remarks that Scott's air in telling the tale was, "in spite of his endeavours to the contrary, as grave as the usual aspect of Laird Nippy of the Peel."

The extreme frequency with which Scott blends with his narrative visions, prophecies, and popular superstitions may fairly lead us to suspect that they were not to his mind absolutely empty things. The Master of Ravenswood's fate is foretold in an old rhyme; a similar rhyme foreshadows the restoration of the heir of Ellangowan to his possessions; a spectre warns Vich Ian Vohr of approaching destruction; and the chief of Clan Alpine is foredoomed by the prophecy of a Highland seer. Instances might be multiplied indefinitely. It cannot of course be supposed that Scott gave a serious assent to such superstitions; but it would seem that he had a vague respect for them, and that he dallied with them in imagination till the boundary between belief and disbelief became

[1] Lockhart, ii. 187.

obscured. He was far too imaginative not to feel that
"there are more things in heaven and earth than are
dreamt of in our philosophy"; and he pleased himself as
a poet and a poetic student of history, by leaving vague
and undefined his own attitude towards the legends which
he found inwoven with the records of fact.   Where occasion demanded he could sift them as well as any man ;
but he delighted rather to leave popular predictions and
Highland second-sight shrouded in a mist.

If this view of Scott's character be correct, he was not,
in his handling of the supernatural, merely giving the
rein to a lawless fancy, but endeavouring to express some
part of the poet's sense of the mystery that encompasses
life.   His manner of doing this is instructive at once
with regard to his own mental constitution and to the
matter upon which he had nourished his mind.   Scott is
nowhere the pure idealist.   The agency by which marvels
are produced is never of that impalpable description which
we find, for example, in Coleridge.   We cannot draw
the line between the powers of earth and the powers
above or under the earth in *Christabel* and *The Ancient
Mariner:* we can in Scott.   He tried once at least to
create a being of the type of Ariel,

> " Something betwixt heaven and hell,
>   Something that neither stood nor fell."

The White Lady of Avenel is a failure that teaches more
than success might have done.   She is a failure, because
when a being who ought to be purely spiritual descends
to pranks and tricks, her charm is gone.   The author's
mistake lay in his attempting to do what nature had not

granted him the power of doing. Given a sorcerer, a soothsayer, a spirit just leaving the body, Scott can use them with wonderful effect; but let the connexion between soul and body be once completely severed, his power seems gone. The best specimen Scott has left of this side of his mind is Wandering Willie's tale in *Redgauntlet*, a masterpiece of the weird and grotesque. Its relation to popular superstition is manifest, but so is its superiority to vulgar *diablerie*. It is at once beyond the ordinary course of nature, and linked to it. Where these conditions are fulfilled, Scott is generally successful in producing the impression he desires to produce. Or he can rouse similar feelings of awe by purely natural means, by the picture of Meg Merrilies over the body of Brown, or of Annie Winnie and Ailsie Gourlay over that of old Alice. But nowhere within the limits of Scott will be found the charm of Shakespeare's Ariel, the majesty of Milton's angels, or the vague suggestiveness of Coleridge's dreamland.

Some may draw the inference that Scott was wanting in delicacy and subtlety. This is true, but true only within limits. His was not the power of the miniature painter on ivory, nor was it that of the visionary prophet. Healthy mind and healthy body were both his; and the best legacy he has left the world is the permanent record of the wholesomeness and manliness of his nature. Carlyle, hopelessly blind to the genius of his great countryman, is fully sensible that he has before him in Scott's works a man. The atmosphere of those works is as fresh at this day as the air of his own hills; and this perhaps is the best guarantee of their permanence. Literary fashions change and pass. The analytical school has had its day of power and influence. It led to a temporary depreciation of work such as that of Scott and Byron. But in the rise of the new school of realism, in the revival of tales of adventure, as well as in the judgments of recent critics, there are signs of reaction; and it seems probable that even Hawthorne, the finest of the analytical school, in spite of his exquisite style and admirable matter, will be forgotten before the less elaborate but really more profound Scott. For, apart from the temporary aberrations of human judgment, there is nothing more sure to live than simple truth and force.

Matthew Arnold quotes Wordsworth's remark about Goethe: "Goethe's poetry was not inevitable enough." Arnold adds: "The remark is striking and true; no line in Goethe, as Goethe said himself, but its maker knew well how it came there." Scott is in this respect like the great German as little as he is like those poets about whom probably Wordsworth was thinking, poets who write in obedience to an overmastering impulse, the δαίμων that speaks through their lips. He is master of himself whether to begin or not; but once he has started he must follow where his creations lead him in defiance of preconceived plan, if any plan has been laid down. "When," says he, in the introduction to *The Fortunes of Nigel*, "When I light on such a character as Bailie Jarvie, or Dalgetty, my imagination brightens, and my conception becomes clearer at every step which I make in his company, although it leads me many a weary mile away from the regular road, and forces me to leap hedge and ditch to get back into the route again. If I resist the temptation, as you advise me, my thoughts become prosy, flat, and dull; I write painfully to myself, and under a consciousness of flagging which makes me flag still more; the sunshine with which fancy had invested the incidents, departs from them, and leaves everything dull and gloomy. I am no more the same author, than the dog in a wheel, condemned to go round and round for hours, is like the same dog merrily chasing his own tail and gambolling in all the frolic of unrestrained freedom."

This element of the inevitable is in part the cause of that irregularity of construction for which Scott has been justly censured. But it is also the spring of the living virtue of his characters. They are no mere puppets whose strings he pulls. They are beings whose development he can partly guide, but whom he must also be at times content to follow. And hence we find that Scott has a subtlety of his own. He has instinctive fineness of touch in the delineation of character. This shows itself sometimes in the language put into the mouth of the character, which changes with unerring taste from Scotch to English as the subject dictates. It appears also in the way in which some apparently trifling hint, dropped casually, and by the reader probably forgotten, is taken up again and made to throw a light upon some actor in the novel. Thus, in chapter xlii. of *Waverley*, Fergus distresses the good Bailie Macwheeble by recklessly flinging his purse, on the eve of the battle of Prestonpans, into the apron of Mrs. Flockhart, and making her his banker or executor according as he may survive or die. Long afterwards, in chapter lxvi., the Bailie reverts to this, in his eyes, most prominent feature of the character of Fergus :—"'I dinna wish the young gentleman ill,' he said, 'but I hope that they that hae got him will keep him, and no let him back to this Hieland border to plague us wi' black-mail, and a' manner o' violent, wrongous, and masterfu' oppression and spoliation, both by himself and others of his causing, sending, and hounding out; *and he couldna tak care o' the siller when he had gotten it neither, but flang it a' into yon idle quean's lap at Edinburgh*—but light come light gane." Again, how admirably, towards the end of *Guy Mannering*, light is thrown upon the character of the usually humble Dominie Sampson :—

"'There is the great Colonel Mannering from the Eastern Indies, who is a man of great erudition considering his imperfect opportunities; and there is, moreover, the great advocate, Mr. Pleydell, who is also a man of great erudition, but who descendeth to trifles unbeseeming thereof; and there is Mr. Andrew Dinmont, whom I do not understand to have possession of much erudition, but who, like the patriarchs of old, is cunning in that which belongeth to flocks and herds. Lastly, there is even I myself, whose opportunities of collecting erudition, as they have been greater than those of the aforesaid valuable persons, have not, if it becomes me to speak, been pre-termitted by me, in so far as my poor faculties have enabled me to profit by them.' . . .

"The reader may observe that, upon this occasion, Sampson was infinitely more profuse of words than he had hitherto exhibited himself. . . . . . And as people seldom speak more than usual without exposing themselves, he gave those whom he addressed plainly to understand that while he deferred implicitly to the opinions and commands, if they chose to impose them, of almost everyone whom he met with, it was under an internal conviction, that in the article of eru-di-ti-on, as he usually pronounced the word, he was infinitely superior to them all put together."

Critics have, almost without a dissenting voice, fixed upon their healthiness as the most prominent and most valuable quality of Scott's novels. There have been and are considerable differences of opinion as to their intrinsic worth; but the verdict has been passed by general agreement that, whether Scott be ranked as a writer high or low, he is at least genuine. The next conspicuous merit of the Waverley Novels is the excellence of their portraiture of character. On this point there has been more dispute; and Carlyle leads the hostile critics with the assertion that Scott is shallow in his delineation of character, working from the skin inward and never getting to the heart. It must suffice here to suggest that what Carlyle mistook for shallowness was really a style and method diametrically opposite to his own. Scott's results are reached without wrestlings and strivings; but it does not follow that they are commonplace. Among the elements which unite to give Scott's characters their charm, humour is perhaps the chief. It is the presence of this quality in greater measure which stamps the novels whose scene is laid in Scotland, or whose characters are drawn from it, with the mark of decisive superiority. Vigour of narrative is likewise characteristic of the Waverley Novels. In the opening of his works Scott often moves slowly, because he is full of other interests besides that of the mere story ; but when he sees fit no one can be more rapid and energetic than he. *Ivanhoe*, up to the siege of Torquil-stone, is a model of narrative prose—the best specimen of this side of his work which Scott has left. Brilliancy and truth of description, variety of situation as well as of character, and that breadth of wisdom, suggestive rather of the statesman than of the novelist, with which he discourses on any subject raised by the course of the story,[1] may also be noted as features of his work. In other respects merit is more mingled with defect. Rapidity of execution results in a style generally simple, natural, and free, but sometimes clumsy and slovenly. It is never laboured, rarely draws attention to itself for its excellence, but occasionally does so for its defects. Rapidity also explains some faults of construction ; but though such faults are not absent, they are on the whole less frequent and prominent than might be expected. A sufficient defence has already been given of this rapidity—it suited the writer better than a more painstaking method of work, and better brought out his strength. To it is due largely the sense of easy mastery with which the novels impress the reader. It is, in short, part of that healthiness which is the first and greatest charm of the Waverley Novels.

The miscellaneous writings, *The Tales of a Grandfather*, *The Life of Napoleon*, and the numerous contributions to periodical literature, must be passed over in silence. But well known as his life is, the facts of Scott's later years cannot be left unnoticed.

---

[1] See the passage about the gipsies quoted by Bagehot from *Guy Mannering*, and his remarks upon it.

The novels were not only a source of delight to readers, they were at the same time a source of wealth to their author. Scott for many years went on adding field to field, completing and perfecting his "romance in stone and lime," and living in Abbotsford the life of boundless hospitality which his imagination delighted to consider the duty of his position as founder and head of a new family. He was during those years as happy, and as deservedly happy, as the chequered course of human life will permit any one to be. But long before that time he had woven round himself toils from which escape was impossible. His partnership with Ballantyne involved him in the crisis which brought down the houses of Hurst, Robinson & Co. in London, and Constable in Edinburgh, and with them that of James Ballantyne & Co. There had been, in 1825, various premonitory mutterings of the tempest; but by the end of the year calm seemed assured; and Scott wrote the spirited song of *Bonnie Dundee* under "the same impulse which makes birds sing when the storm has blown over."[1] In the beginning of the following year it burst in good earnest. Scott was ruined. He was personally liable for £117,000, great part of it represented by "accommodation" bills for which no consideration had ever been received. He had been deeply wrong. He had been rash, even reckless, in his manner of trading. He had allowed this system of interchange of bills to go on unchecked; he had even stimulated it and in a manner made it necessary by indulgence in the pernicious habit of anticipating profits and drawing upon the future. His errors are patent;

[1] *Journal*, December 22, 1825.

but splendidly he redeemed them. He could of course, like any other debtor, have shielded himself under the law of bankruptcy. He declined to do so. He asked of the creditors time, and with time he was sanguine of clearing off all the crushing burden laid upon him. The "Great Unknown," now become, in his own phrase, "the Too-well Known," spent the remainder of his life in a dauntless struggle to discharge his debts. He shortened his days in the effort, and died with his end unaccomplished; but between insurance, copyrights, and the generous exertions of Lockhart, the whole was in the end cleared off, and in 1847 the last creditor of Sir Walter Scott was paid in full.

In November, 1825, he had begun a *Journal*, suggested by that of Byron. It is freely quoted by Lockhart and has recently been published *in extenso*. This should not be neglected in a criticism of Scott's works; for between it and the fragment of autobiography he adds to his gallery of portraits the noblest figure of all, himself. Lockhart's almost matchless *Life* supplements them; and together they place Scott alongside of Johnson as one of the two best depicted figures in our literature. The *Journal* begins in prosperity; soon the clouds gather; the crash comes; and then it leads us through gloom and disaster—shattered fortunes, dying wife, failing strength, overworn brain; but manly resolution and unswerving sense of duty are stronger than all. There are some passages of touching beauty; the whole is a most mournful tragedy. At the close the only words possible seem to be those of Kent over Lear :—

"O, let him pass! he hates him much
That would upon the rack of this tough world
Stretch him out longer."

The virtues of Scott were many, his faults few and
venial. Those who were dependent upon him loved
him with a devotion which his care for them had well
deserved. His servants were all ready to follow him
in adversity as in prosperity; some whom he felt bound
to dismiss would take no discharge; they served not
for money but for affection. About a poor hunch-
backed tailor, William Goodfellow, Lockhart tells a story
for the moral credit of which it might be well worth
while to barter the glory of the Waverley Novels. "Not
long after he had completed his work at Abbotsford,
little Goodfellow fell sick, and as his cabin was near
Chiefswood, I had many opportunities of observing the
Sheriff's kind attention to him in his affliction. I can
never forget, in particular, the evening on which the
poor tailor died. When Scott entered the hovel he
found every thing silent, and inferred from the looks of
the good women in attendance that their patient had
fallen asleep, and that they feared his sleep was the
final one. He murmured some syllables of kind regret;—
at the sound of his voice the dying tailor unclosed his
eyes, and eagerly and wistfully sat up, clasping his hands
with an expression of rapturous gratefulness and devotion, that, in the midst of deformity, disease, pain, and
wretchedness, was at once beautiful and sublime. He
cried with a loud voice, 'the Lord bless and reward
you,' and expired with the effort."

The profound sadness of Scott's declining years seems

a terrible retribution for faults so trivial; yet on full consideration, now that he has gone to his rest, it is difficult to wish the facts other than they were. He was great in his works, great in his prosperous life, but greatest of all in his closing years of adversity. Lockhart finely quotes, "The glory dies not, and the grief is past."

GLOSSARY.

A', *all.*
Aboon or abune, *above.*
Ae, *one.*
Aik, *oak.*
Ain, *own.*
Airt, *quarter, point of the compass.*
Aith, *oath.*
A-jee, *to one side.*
Ane, *one.*
Anis, *ones.*
Areist, *legal arrestment.*
Auld, *old.*
Awin, *own.*

Bairn, *child,*
Baith, *both.*
Bane, *bone.*
Bang, *rush.*
Bannock, *a kind of oat-cake.*
Rauckie-bird, *bat.*
Bauld, *bold.*
Baw, *ball.*
Bedeen, *quickly.*
Beet, *add fuel to.*
Begouth, *began.*
Beik, *warm.*
Ben, *the inner room.*
Bent, *a kind of coarse grass, an open field.*
Berne, *man.*
Big, *build.*
Bing, *a heap, a boarded enclosure for holding grain.*
Birneist, *burnished.*
Bis, *hiss like hot iron plunged into water.*
Black-a-vic'd, *black visaged.*
Black-mail, *a tax paid to freebooters to secure property from pillage.*
Blads, *pieces, fragments.*
Blashy, *deluging.*

Blate, *bashful.*
Blattering, *rattling.*
Blaw, *blow.*
Blink, *glance.*
Blude or bluid, *blood.*
Bonny, *pretty.*
Bot or but, *without, only.*
Bourd, *jest.*
Bousteous, *boisterous.*
Brae, *hill.*
Braid, *broad.*
Brak or brake, *broke.*
Branglit, *shook, menaced.*
Braw, *pretty.*
Brawnd, *brawn.*
Breeks, *breeches.*
Brunstane, *brimstone.*
Buik, *book.*
Buir or bure, *bore.*
Buirdly, *sturdy.*
Busk, *adorn.*
Buss, *bush.*
But, *see bot.*
But, *the outer room.*
Byast, *biased.*

Ca', *call, drive.*
Caird, *tinker.*
Caller or cawler, *fresh.*
Canny, *quiet.*
Canty, *merry.*
Carl, *fellow.*
Cauld, *cold.*
Causey, *causeway, street.*
Channerin', *fretting, grumbling.*
Channoun, *canon.*
Chekin, *chicken.*
Clachan, *a small village.*
Claith, *cloth.*
Cleugh, *a hollow between steep banks.*
Cleir, *clear, bright.*

Clok, *beetle.*
Coppare, *cupbearer.*
Cour, *cower.*
Couthie, *friendly.*
Crack, *talk.*
Crakt, *pealed.*
Cramasie, *crimson.*
Cranreuch, *hoar-frost.*
Crap, *crop.*
Cray, *cry.*
Crock, *an old ewe past bearing.*
Cubiculare, *groom of the bed-chamber.*
Culum, *tail.*
Cure, *care.*
Cutty, *short.*

Daft, *mad.*
Dauis, *dawns.*
Daundering, *sauntering.*
Deid, *dead, death.*
Deil, *devil.*
Deme, *dame.*
Ding, *beat.*
Dinna, *do not.*
Dinsome, *noisy.*
Dissagyist, *disguised.*
Divot, *turf.*
Divot seat, *a seat at the door of a cottage made of "divots."*
Dool, *sorrow.*
Dousser, *more sedate.*
Dowie, *melancholy.*
Draif, *drove.*
Dreip, *drip.*
Drib, *drop.*
Droich, *a dwarf.*
Ducht, *could.*
Dule, *sorrow.*
Dwyning, *pining, fading.*

Een, *eyes.*
Eerie or eirie, *filled with superstitious fear, fitted to produce such fear.*
Elrich, *ghastly, preternatural.*
Ewe-buchtin', *milking the ewes in the pen.*

Fa', *fall, befall.*
Fae, *foe.*
Fand, *found.*
Fash, *trouble.*
Fasheous, *troublesome.*
Fear, *fair, smooth.*
Fecfull, *pithy.*
Feckless, *feeble.*

Feckly, *mostly.*
Feggs, *a paltry oath, faith.*
Feiralie, *fierily.*
Ferly, *marvel.*
Ferss, *fierce.*
Flae, *flay.*
Flaucht, *flash.*
Flee, *fly.*
Fleetching, *flattering.*
Flure, *floor.*
Flyting, *scolding.*
Fou or fow, *full, tipsy.*
Fouth, *abundance.*
Fowk, *folk.*
Frae, *from.*
Frak, *hurry.*
Fu', *full.*
Fuffe, *puff.*
Fyl'd, soiled.

Gaberlunzie, *a wallet; hence, the beggar who carries the wallet.*
Gae, *go, gave.*
Gaist or ghaist, *ghost.*
Gane, *gone.*
Gang, *go.*
Gappocks, *gobbets.*
Gar, *cause.*
Garnassing, *garnishing.*
Gash, *sagacious, talkative.*
Gate, *way.* Tak' the gate, *begin to go about.*
Gaun, *going.*
Geyre, *gear.*
Geyzed, *leaky for want of moisture.*
Gie, *give.*
Gif, *if.*
Gin, *if.*
Girn, *grin.*
Gled, *kite.*
Glint, *glance.*
Glower, *stare.*
Goud, *gold.*
Gowan, *daisy.*
Gowdspink, *goldfinch.*
Gowfer, *golfer.*
Greislie, *grisly.*
Grew, *shiver.*
Grit, *great.*
Gruntill, *snout.*
Grymin', *sprinkling.*
Gud or gudis, *goods.*
Gude or guid, *good.*
Gudewife, *mistress of a house.*
Gudlie, *goodly.*
Gurly, *angry, stormy.*

Had, *hold.*
Hae, *have.*
Ha'-house, *mansion.*
Haiss, *has, have.*
Haith, *faith (an oath).*
Happit, *covered.*
Hard, *heard.*
Hauver-meal, *oatmeal.*
Hecht, *promised.*
Heeze, *lift, aid.*
Heich, *high.*
Heid, *head.*
Herry, *harry, rob.*
Heugh, *crag.*
Heyghlie, *highly.*
Hing, *hang.*
Hint, *behind.*
Hip, *miss.*
Hirplin, *moving crazily, creeping.*
Hoill or hole, *whole.*
Hoist, *cough.*
Hulie, *slowly, gently.*

Ilk or ilka, *each, every.*
Ingan, *onion.*
Ingle, *fire.*
Ither, *other.*

Jimp, *slender.*
Jo, *sweetheart.*

Kail, *colewort.*
Kail-yard, *cabbage-garden.*
Kaim or kame, *comb.*
Keek, *peep.*
Kemping, *striving.*
Ken, *know.*
Kep, *catch.*
Kimmer, *gossip.*
Knak, *gibe.*
Know, *knoll.*
Ky, *cows.*
Kyste, *chest, coffin.*

Laigh, *low.*
Laip, *lap.*
Laith, *loth.*
Landward, *rustic.*
Landward town, *farm buildings remote from others.*
Lat, *let.*
Late-wake, *another form of 'lyke-wake.'*
Lave, *rest, remainder.*
Laverock, *lark.*

Leeze me, *dear is to me.* Leeze me on, *my blessing on.*
Leven, *lawn.*
Lift, *sky.*
Lightly, *slight in love.*
Lilting, *singing cheerfully.*
Lintie, *linnet.*
Lo'e, *love.*
Loun, *a worthless fellow.*
Loup, *leap.*
Lowisit, *unyoked.*
Lufe, *love.*
Lyart, *grizzled.*
Lyeff, *life.*
Lykewake, *the watching of a dead body.*
Lyre, *flesh.*

Mair, *more.*
Maist, *most, almost.*
Man or maun, *must.*
Mane, *moan.*
Maut, *malt.*
Mearelie, *merrily.*
Meikle, *big.*
Menis, *esteem, make known.*
Micht, *might.*
Mirk, *dark.*
Mishanter, *misfortune.*
Misthryue, *thrive badly.*
Molde, *ground, mould.*
Mon, *must.*
Moul', *mould.*
Muckle, *large, much.*
Mumper, *mumbler, mincing speaker.*
Mutchkin, *pint.*
Mydding, *dunghill.*

Na, *not.*
Nae, *no.*
Nare, *nor.*
Nay-says, *refusals.*
Neep, *turnip.*
Neist or niest, *next.*
Nicht, *night.*
Nippy, *niggard.*
Nocht, *not, nought.*
Nuk, *nook.*

O'ercome, *overplus.*
Ony, *any.*
Or, *ere.*
Orrow, *spare.*
Owr, ower, or owre, *over, too.*
Oxtar, *arm-pit.*

Papyngo, *parrot.*
Parafle, *embroidery, ostentatious display.*
Pawky, *artful.*
Peltrie, *trash.*
Pentit, *painted.*
Pertyde, *parted.*
Pickle, *a small quantity.*
Plainstanes, *pavement.*
Plouckie, *covered with pimples.*
Plwch, *plough.*
Poin'd, *distrained, seized.*
Poortith, *poverty.*
Poppling, *bubbling.*
Pou, *pull.*
Powsodie, *sheep's-head broth.*
Prievin', *proving, tasting.*
Puir, *poor.*
Pyne, *pain.*

Quat, *quit, let go.*
Quean, *wench.*
Queir, *choir.*
Quha, *who.*
Quhare, *where.*
Quharefor, *wherefor.*
Quhat, *what.*
Quhen, *when.*
Quhile, *until, while, so long as.*
Quhilk, *which.*
Quhowbeit, *howbeit.*
Quhyte, *white.*
Quo or quod, *quoth.*

Raise, *rose.*
Rang, *reigned.*
Reesting, *drying.*
Reid, *red.*
Reik, *smoke.*
Richt, *right.*
Rift, *belch.*
Rin, *run.*
Ripe, *poke.*
Rock, *distaff.*
Rokelay, *cloak.*
Roughies, *torches.*
Row, *roll.*
Rowth, *plenty.*
Ruch, *rough.*
Rude, *cross.*
Rung, *staff.*
Rycht, *right.*
Ryue, *burst.*

Sackless, *innocent.*
Sae, *so.*

Saft, *soft.*
Sair, *sore.*
Scar, *cliff.*
Schaip, *make go.*
Scherwe, *serve.*
Schiep, *sheep.*
Schiftis, *shifts.*
Schowt, *shout.*
Scour, *draught.*
Scud, *hurry on.*
Seally, *silly, weak.*
Seasit, *legally conveyed.*
Seware, *steward.*
Sey, *try, prove.*
Sey-piece, *a piece of work executed as a proof of skill.*
Shaw, *a wood in a hollow.*
Sheugh, *ditch.*
Shogle, *dangle.*
Shynand, *shining.*
Siccan, *such.*
Siller, *silver, money.*
Skaith, *harm.*
Sklent, *slope.*
Skyte, *a smart blow.*
Slap, *a pass.*
Sled, *slid.*
Sleekit, *smooth, cunning.*
Sma', *small.*
Sned, *to lop off.*
Snod, *neat.*
Snool, *to submit tamely.*
Somegate, *somehow.*
Sowld, *should.*
Spat, *spot.*
Spaul, *shoulder.*
Spier, *inquire.*
Sponk or spunk, *spark.*
Spraing, *tint.*
Spune, *spoon.*
Spurtill, *a stick to stir porridge.*
Starn, *star.*
Staw, *stole.*
Steek, *to shut.*
Steird, *drove.*
Stottis, *oxen.*
Stoup, *a flagon, a prop.*
Streikit, *stretched, laid out (of a dead body).*
Stryckis, *strikes.*
Sulde, *should.*
Syde, *long.*
Syke, *rill.*
Syne, *next, then.*

Taiken, *token.*

Takkand, *taking.*
Tantonie bell, *St. Antony's bell.*
Tappit hen, *crested hen, a measure containing three quarts.*
Targatting, *a sort of embroidery.*
Tee, *the nodule of earth from which the ball is driven in golf.*
Teind, *tithe.*
Tent, *care.*
Thae, *these.*
Thesaurare, *treasurer.*
Thocht, *though, thought.*
Thoom, *thumb.*
Thow, *thaw.*
Thrang, *busy, crowded.*
Thraw, *twist.*
Thud, *a loud intermittent noise.*
Tine, *to be lost.*
Tippenny, *two-penny.*
Toddlin', *tottering.*
Tocher, *dowry.*
Tow, *to lower by a rope.*
Trews, *trousers.*
Tuke, *took.*
Tulchan, *a calf's skin stuffed with straw, used to induce a cow to give her milk : hence applied to bishops who held the title of the office, but were only the means of getting the temporalities for some lay person.*
Tyll, *to.*
Tynt, *lost.*

Unco, *wonderful.*
Unsell, *worthless.*
Usit, *used, accustomed.*

Vissart, *visor.*
Vogie, *cheerful.*

Wa', *wall.*
Wae, *woe.*
Wait, *know.*
Wallop, *to move quickly and clumsily.*
Waly, *alas.*
Warstle, *strife.*
Wat, *wet.*
Waukin', *awake.*
Wean, *child.*
Wear or weir, *war.*
Wee, *little.*
Weet, *to make wet.*
Weill, *well.*
Whang, *slice.*
Whiles, *sometimes.*
Whin, *gorse.*
Whisht, *hush.*
Whop, *whip, snatch.*
Wicht, *man, person.*
Wiltu, *wilt thou.*
Wow, *woo.*
Wrack or wrak, *wreck, trash.*
Wud, *mad.*
Wyit or wyte, *blame.*
Wympler, *lock of hair.*
Wysing, *directing cunningly.*

Yird, *earth.*
Ynewcht, *enough.*
Yowes, *ewes.*

Zit, *yet.*

INDEX.

PRINTED BY ROBERT MACLEHOSE, UNIVERSITY PRESS, GLASGOW.